# *THE DEVIL'S VOICE*

***DON*** [illegible]

This is a true story [illegible] ted murder. A journey [illegible] ied, petite and defencele[illegible] year old little girl to an eighteen year old teenager.

The battle to overcome the scars of my hidden past and to endure the painful steps in order to unlock and tell the memories of horror, in the hope of making a success of my life.

# *Acknowledgements*

I am sharing my story in the hope of helping someone else take positive steps and not to let the upsets of their past destroy their lives like it had done mine until now.

For those poor individuals who have suffered from childhood abuse, here is hoping that I can set up support to help you.

I would like to thank my husband Bobby for his support; his kindness and patience has been fantastic.

I would like to express my undying gratitude to my therapist who has never given up on me.

I would like to pray for anyone that has experienced some of the traumatic events that I have and ended their lives.

In advance, I would like to thank anyone that reads this book and supports what I am asking.

## *Introduction*

I grew up in Salford and had five brothers and one sister; we lived in a tower block of flats on the first floor. There were other tower blocks that were all roughly fourteen stories high. This was where I was born and continued to live until the age of twelve.

Our flat had three bedrooms, a bathroom, lounge, kitchen and a long lobby, looking back it was quite a dismal place to live but my childhood days were happy or at least this is what I believed.

There was never a dull moment with the amount of people living in the flat. I shared a bedroom with my sister and younger brother. My four other brothers shared a bedroom and my mum and dad had their own.

In the sixties and early seventies nobody who lived in the area had much money and seemed to have large families like ours.

Every Thursday we would have a chippy tea and drink fizzy pop as a treat. We would squash together on the carpet and watch Top Cat on the TV; we'd have to put up a good fight to get a decent spot. One of my brothers would chirp up with "Take your shadow off my spot.'

Christmas times were always magical. We all used to wake up to loads of presents and we always got a tangerine. My dad was determined that we wouldn't have a childhood like he had. He came from a large family and his dad used to beat him often. He never celebrated Christmas or birthdays as his family had no money. The first ever card and present he received was when he was twenty one years old. As he got older and had a family of his own, he swore no child of his would ever have a childhood like he had. I think that's why we got a tangerine each Christmas; this would have been such a luxury for him when he was a child.

Although we never had much money, we were all well fed and had clothes on our backs, quite often these would have been hand me downs but we never gave this a second thought. We were never spoilt but we did get treats on a weekly basis, usually sweets from the shop or occasionally I would get a princess headset or some other small toy. We would always have a holiday each year. Usually we went to Cornwall or Lands' End and stayed in a caravan. I will never forget travelling in the car. Mum and dad would be in the front and the seven of us would be in the back crammed like sardines. Of course, back then there were no laws about seatbelts or how many people were travelling in one vehicle.

My memories of my childhood seemed sweet, we were always well looked after. My mum always seemed to be there sharing her love with me, my sister and five brothers, she always had time for all of us. She was not a firm mum and probably naive in a lot of ways but we all knew if she was angry at us by the tone in her voice. If any of us did something wrong her voice was enough to get the guilt flowing and get at your conscience, enough to make you own up and apologise. . My dad on the other hand was firm and would take his belt to you if my mother ever had to report disobedient behaviour back to him. Dad worked long hours but always made time for us and showered us with plenty of love and affection. I have so much respect for my mum and used to for my dad.

As a child I was always out playing games with my friends, our favourites included hopscotch, tag and British Bulldog. Virtually everyone in the neighbourhood at all ages used to join us when playing British bulldog. I used to find stones and draw hopscotch on the paving flags. Back in the 60s/70s there was no technology so all children played outside as children should, creating new games and getting plenty of fresh air and exercise.

I grew up in what I thought was a very loving family, a family who stood by each other. I've always thought of myself as close to my siblings and as we got older we stayed in touch and got together for family events. However, for some reason I have never felt complete, like there has always been something there that prevented sincere happiness in my life.

I have always considered myself to be a 'normal'

person that takes life's knockbacks on the chin and bounces back, that's who I thought I was. I have come to realise that that's not actually the truth. The truth is from a very young age, possibly five, maybe even younger; I have been raped on more than four occasions, and have been physically, emotionally and mentally abused. Looking back, I was almost murdered on more than one occasion. For many years after, I lived in fear and unable to talk about what happened or confide in anyone. My past memories were so painful and being unable to face such horror, I locked the memories away in a sealed box in my mind. After all, it was my fault these horrible events happened and this is what I was made to believe.

Now at 55 years old the sealed box that I hid so well has started to crack open. With each crack that appears I am beginning to see that I have had a past that seems unrealistic, unfair and filled with horrible events, events that I have never been able to face. I am now reliving my past which has caused me so much heartache and despair.

I am going to tell you about my past experiences in detail. I find this upsetting to write about and I am battling with the courage to complete this. Writing about these events has and is still helping me through such a traumatic time in my life and has made me recognise that what has happened is not my fault and the fault of evil psychopaths who took advantage and stole the innocence of a little girl.

I am currently seeing a therapist; my therapist tells me I have got complex PTSD (post-traumatic stress disorder). I am sure that there are people out there who are battling traumatic experiences and not had any support in dealing with this.

## Contents

## Chapter 1

## Childhood background and the gateway to hell

My mum and dad have raised seven children. All my siblings and I have all got good manners and have been brought up to respect others and be thankful for what we have. I am the second youngest child; I have four older brothers Tim, Malcolm, Mark and Jake. My sister Jane is one and a half years older than me, and my youngest brother Charles is one and a half years younger.

We never really had much when I was a child but I was always well fed and had fairly decent clothes, even the pass me downs were of good quality. We were cared for well and always felt loved by my mum and dad. I can't really remember any point in my childhood that I have ever felt deprived and I suppose our wealth was the riches of love and not material gains.

We lived in a three bedroom flat, my four older brothers shared a bedroom, my mum and dad had their own bedroom and me, my sister and younger brother shared a room. We had a long hallway, a kitchen, lounge and we had one small gas fire that was in the lounge and was meant to keep the entire flat warm. It was horrible in winter, especially the mornings, the whole flat was freezing and we had ice on the insides of the windows. I would get out of bed in my vest and knickers and race towards the lounge and stand in front of the gas fire to get warm.

There was always washing on the clothes maiden, which had become a permanent part of the furniture, it was the only place my mum could get anything dry apart from going to the launderette. She would fold clean washing and put it into piles to be put away in the bedrooms but the washing never seemed to get put away and the flat was always cluttered.

In my bedroom, the ceiling had a damp patch in the corner; this was unsightly and always caught my eye when I went in and out of my bedroom. There were no such things as duvets, we had blankets on our beds that were very scratchy but we had plenty of them to keep us warm at night.

We had a lemon and white kitchenette in the kitchen where my mum kept the food, we didn't have a fridge or freezer back then and sometimes when I poured milk on my cereal in the morning it would be sour and come out of the glass bottle in lumps, if the milk was off we had toast if the milkman was late.

The flat was not the tidiest of places; this is probably because there was so many of us living there. We had a huge black and white television in the lounge. I remember every time the news came on I used to hide behind the television because I truly thought that the news reader was talking to me and that he could see me, his eyes seemed to be looking right at me and I was such a shy girl. I think my mum used to tell me that he could see me so that I would get dressed faster.

Although we had a settee it was a rarity if I managed to sit on it before the spaces were taken up by the rest of my family and on the occasions when I did get a place my older brothers would usually pull me off so that they could sit on it. Most of the time I sat on the floor near the fire to keep warm. Sometimes when my mum sat down I would go and sit on her knee to get a cuddle.

Most people lived in flats like ours, the flats were fourteen storey blocks high and the area was surrounded by these tower blocks. We didn't have a lot; I suppose when I look back we had the basics the same as everyone else. We weren't what you would call poor but we certainly weren't rich or well off or in no worse state then other families.

I used to go to Kersal Primary School which was about ten minutes' walk from our flat, my mum would walk us there and pick us up once school had finished. It was always hectic because there were that many of us and there would always be one of us that got told off for dawdling behind.

I liked school because I used to get a small bottle of milk with a straw in it, in the summer the milk used to be warm and in the winter I would have to break through the ice and the milk seemed to have a watery taste to it. At play time I used to draw hopscotch on the floor with a stone and my friends and I would play. Other times we would play skipping, two children at each end of the skipping rope and one of us in the middle jumping over the rope. When the rope caught your foot someone else would have a turn in the middle and there was always a queue of children lining up to have a go. I used to have so much fun and had plenty of other kids to play with. When it was mid-morning break I would go to the tuck shop and buy some potato puffs with my snack money, I think this was the best part of the school day. The school always had art work on the walls and I was sure that there were some really clever children at school because some of the art work on display was really good.

I loved Christmas time at school, taking part in singing the Christmas carols; my favourite carol was "Once in Royal David's City". We used to have a small Christmas party in my class, everyone got a Christmas cracker and we would have sandwiches and cakes. My whole class made Christmas cards for our families in the morning and in the afternoon on the last day we had an early finish. I got excited because I knew that I would be breaking up for the Christmas holidays.

After school I was always allowed to play out as long as one of my older brothers was watching us. They told mum that they would watch us but they always tried to find ways to ditch us. I would be the first one to tell mum if they tried this and they would get told off and be made to look after us. I played out for hours at a time, there was always someone to play with and I was never bored.

There was no such thing as a mobile phone, come to think about it, there were no electrical games like they have now. Back then, kids used to be kids and it was very rare you saw another kid that was overweight. We didn't have the chance to be overweight; we were all active and running round playing. Nobody wanted to stay indoors as we wouldn't have had as much fun on our own.

I used to play with my dolls and pram when I was inside. My brothers would sometimes torment me, usually for fun but sometimes they would go too far and my sensitive side would take hold leading me to tears. These are all happy memories that are shared and laughed about later on in life. These memories are healthy and the kind of which every child should have and be able treasure as they get older, after all we are just a normal family.

On school nights I had to come in when it would start getting dark, at the weekends I was allowed to play out all day, these were good days. I used to get really hungry during the day and would ask mum if I could have a jam or marmalade butty, sometimes I would have a banana butty. The simplicity of the food that we ate was so enjoyable and cost effective.

At tea time we would have stew or similar meals; I didn't really like stew and would ask dad if I could have something else. He would never gave in to this and always said no, he would never force me to eat it but would say if you don't eat it now, I would have it for supper and if I didn't eat it at supper I would get it for breakfast. I wouldn't be allowed anything else to eat until I ate my tea. I suppose it was hard work cooking for so many and not having much money would have been the reason we all had to eat what we were given. There was nothing that was harsh about this and this prevented any of us being so called "fussy eaters".

I got on with all my family even though we had our squabbles and I seemed to get teased a lot. My older brothers were good to me, apart from Malcolm who I always had a fear of, my brother Malcolm who was the second oldest, eight years older than me. Malcolm was always a rebel and he seemed to get in trouble often and more than any of us. His offences ranged from getting into a lot of fights, stealing or being destructive. He was always rough and ready and had lots of friends.

He wasn't like my other brothers and somehow seemed to really get a kick and enjoy upsetting me and my sister. I usually tried to avoid him and tried my best to stay out of his way. He would always take his tormenting ways too far and make my sister and I cry. He would continually get a telling off from my parents when he did this, but this didn't stop him.

You see, the kind of tormenting he did in front of others just seemed like he was teasing us and trying to make us cry. The real torment was a dark secret which I dared not shared with anyone. He made me and my sister do things to him against our will, he would then convince us to keep it a secret.

Malcolm seemed to have some kind of a way with me that led me to believe that what he was doing is acceptable and normal; he also had a way of getting to me as he made it clear that something would happen to me if I told anyone about his game.

He seemed to have the power of control and because I was so scared of him I daren't tell anyone as his temper was so unpredictable. He always warned my sister and me not to tell anyone and to 'keep our gobs shut.' I think it was the threatening way in which he said this and his day to day behaviour that put the fear of god into both of us and convinced us that it was better to keep quiet.

Malcolm told us that he had made a game up and only my sister and I could play it with him. Each time we played this game he made us promise that we wouldn't tell anyone about our secret; it was always said in malice to make certain that we knew it was best to keep his dirty secret quiet. I was just a little girl and knew there was no way anybody would believe me over him, and besides how could I tell somebody else when I didn't truly understand myself what he was doing to me?

It all started when my mum got a part time evening job, I can't really remember my age at this time, I think I was eight or younger but I know I was at such a young age where I didn't know what I was doing. He called it the rock game, he started by making us touch his private area and then we had to hold his penis and move our hands up and down. He would make my sister and I masturbate him, my sister would have been around 9 years old, just as young and innocent as I.

I have never forgotten how he used to make me masturbate him until I cried because my arms were aching; at this point he would make my sister switch places until she too cried in pain.

I remember him lying on the floor with his pants half way down to his knees, his eyes were always closed and his face screwed up. He would say! "Do it faster! Do it faster!" When I couldn't do anymore he would get my sister to take over, or she would start and I would take over until he finished. I used to think he had wet himself, but looking back most of the time he had actually ejaculated onto our hands.

My sister and I didn't like playing this game, we didn't really know what we were doing but we knew that it hurt arms and we didn't take any pleasure in it. My arms would be burning and feel so achy and I would cry with the pain, but he wouldn't let us stop.

He made this into a competition and used to say that the one who made it harder would get some money. We never got any money, nor did any of us want any, I for one just wanted to get out of his way and didn't want to end up playing another game.

When my mum went to work, Malcolm and my other older brothers had to babysit us for a few hours. I used to dread it as Malcolm would not allow us to have a choice and we had to play his stupid horrible game, this was away from my other brothers. I don't really know what my other brothers were doing at these times, probably in the lounge watching TV or playing music.

As you can imagine the house was always fairly noisy and it was not unusual for one or two of us to disappear into our bedrooms as this was normal.

His game developed into a regular thing and I used to dread my mum going out. I didn't find his game disgusting as I was too young and innocent to understand, all I knew it was something that hurt me and made me cry. I didn't like playing, neither did my sister. He seemed to have a knack of making it clear what would happen if we told anyone about his secret.

I know of at least one occasion my brother Malcolm put his hand down the front of my knickers and touched me inappropriately. I was too young to understand his actions but I remember it hurting and being told "You dare tell anyone!" it wasn't just the tone of his voice that I feared, it was also the way he looked at me.

On some occasions I began to rebel, thinking that I would be safe whilst my parents were present. He would show me what he was capable of by tripping me up so I would fall and hurt my head and knees. His response, "Whoops! I told you accidents would happen." It was his way of saying that he would hurt me if I dared tell. I was scared of him and for so many reasons.

My brother has always been a rebel and had a reputation as being a hard nut; he seemed to be known as the black sheep of the family because of the trouble he got himself in.

I don't honestly know what age I was when all this started, that period of my life is a blur, what I do know is it became a regular chore and I dreaded the thought of my mum going to work and leaving me with him. Within minutes of her leaving he would have found a way to get us alone, no matter what I did to avoid being alone with him. I can't understand how he got these opportunities without others knowing what he was doing.

Afterwards he would let us pick what we wanted to watch on the TV, it just seemed so normal to him, but for my sister and I it was like a chore that we hated doing and had become part of a regular routine. I had no idea of what pleasure he got out of it. Even as a kid, I found the smell that was left on my hand repulsive, the kind of stench that would leave me feeling sick.

Every Friday my brothers took it in turns to by ice creams, this particular week it must have been Malcolm's turn. My younger brother, sister and I kept asking him to go to the ice cream van before it left. He said he would if me and my sister went to our bedroom and stayed there until he shouted us, otherwise he wouldn't buy us one.

After some time he shouted us both to get our ice cream, we walked out the bedroom and there he was stood with our ice creams. Being the game player that he was, he must have bought an empty cornet, filled it with shaving foam so that it looked like an ice cream and then gave it to me. I just thought it was an ice cream, why would I think any different? I put this in my mouth and all I could taste was soap, I cried and threw it on the floor and told him I was going to tell mum what he had done, he laughed and found this highly amusing.

My older brother Tim told him to stop being horrible and called him a tight pig. Malcolm passed me the real ice cream and said that he was only joking and stop being a cry baby. I got so mad at him and threw the whole ice cream at him in a paddy and then ran to my room sulking. Normally I would not remember silly tricks like this, but even now at 55 years old this memory has scared me for life because of what happened next.

I was lying on my bed sulking and had been there for some time as I fell asleep. My brother Malcolm woke me up by teasing and tormenting me. The bedroom was almost pitched black, it was cold and I could see a slither of light through the doorway as the hall light was on. I felt groggy because he had just awoken me, I told him to go away and leave me alone. I just thought he was teasing as normal until he started to get really rough, this was different from his usual tormenting.

He pinned my arms above my head and then sat on top of me with his knees pressing on my shoulders and chest. I thought my lungs were broken. I could hardly breathe with his weight on top of me, he felt so heavy, and I thought he was trying to crush me. I was smothered under his weight and couldn't move. He got his penis out and waved it on my face, it was touching my cheek and then my nose and lips. He told me to open my mouth and suck it; the smell was horrible and stunk of urine. He tried to prize my mouth open but I tried with all my might to keep it shut tight. He must have known that he couldn't make me do this so he gave up trying. I remember panicking because I could not take a breath in, his weight was crushing the life out of me. I knew I had to get him off me. I mustered up the words “get off me,” I had to gasp for breath in between each word as I could only get one word out at a time. I struggled to get air in my lungs and tried fighting him until the strength in my tiny body began to fade.

I felt him turn me on my side, suddenly I gasped for air. I was so relieved that I could finally breathe. As my breathing became more regular and easier he suddenly grabbed me again and locked me into a position where I become powerless to move, he was so much bigger and stronger than I was.

He pinned me down on my back, one arm under my shoulders and one around my waist; his legs were tight around my legs. His hand moved down and he began to touch me down below with his fingers, then he pulled me right back to him and told me to keep quiet. I was so scared and this was something totally different from my other experiences. I was convinced this would be the time he was going to kill me. I kept screaming at him to get of me and that I’m going to tell, but these words were silent and would not come out. I felt a horrible pain and burning sensation; I was screaming in my head and so desperately hoping someone would hear my silent screams. I was looking at the bedroom door which was slightly ajar and the light from the hallway partially lighting the dark room.

Suddenly my little brother opened the door and told Malcolm to stop hurting me or else he would tell mum, then just disappeared out the room. I continued to stare at the door. He didn't stop and I am sure that my little brother didn't know what Malcolm was doing to me as he was younger than me. I had no idea of what he was doing, all I understood was the pain he was inflicting on me.

I looked at the damp patch on my bedroom ceiling and stared at this for a distraction. I cried and managed to voice the words that were going round my head "Get off me! Get off me! You're hurting me! Get off! Get off!" He just kept telling me to shut up and stop being such a baby, keep quiet.

It seemed like I was there for hours and that it would never end. With each thrust I thought he was slowly killing me; the pain was unbearable, it felt horrible and I felt so alone. I have never been so scared.

Eventually he stopped and this hard thing inside me went soft, afterwards he told me that I was a dirty bitch and should be ashamed of myself. I was sobbing, I felt so broke inside and out. I didn't know what was happening or what he had done. I screamed out at him "I'm going to tell dad that you tried to kill me." I didn't know it was rape, just that I was hurting so bad and felt so scared of him.

He pushed me really hard and carried on pushing and pushing me, he wouldn't let me pass him. He used my hair to pull my head back, he seemed to be right in my face and the look in his eyes made my heart beat so fast, I could feel my heart pounding.

Everything became so distant and my whole tiny body was shaking. He told me that if I told anyone it would be me that would get into trouble for what I had done, and kept telling me how dirty I was, “Keep your mouth shut or I will get you again you dirty little bitch.”

It wasn’t long after that my mum came home from work. I was so desperate to tell her about my brother hurting me, I wanted her to cuddle me so badly and in my head I was begging her to notice my pain. Instead I went to her and cried and told her I felt poorly. I was so worked up and just wanted to scream the words but it was like they were stuck and entwined in the knot I had in my stomach.

Malcolm was staring at me as I was being cuddled by my mum, his piercing eyes looking at me, sending the message of terror through my whole body. At this point I didn’t feel safe in my mum’s arms. I sat on my mum’s knee and got a five minute cuddle and then was sent to bed. My mum tucked me in and I felt the itchy blankets on my skin. As my mum started to walk out my bedroom, Malcolm stood in the doorway, although he did not say a word, the look in his eyes reminded me to keep quite.

The hall light was left on and I looked up at the damp patch on my bedroom ceiling. After staring at the shape for a while a face appeared, I was sure it was the face of the devil and the more I stared at this, the more I was convinced my brother had put him there to watch me and make sure I kept quiet. I know now this was my imagination, but back then it seemed so real and I was petrified of it.

After this, I started to wet the bed. I found myself scared of going to bed. Each night I would lie there and look at the devils face on the bedroom ceiling and cringe with so much fear. I would try to hide under the bed covers so that I didn't have to look at it. I would keep pulling the bed covers down slightly and would keep peeping to see if it was still there. As I peaked at its haunting face, the eyes became life like, it was watching me!

Sometimes I would tell it to go away and promised I would keep quiet and that I would be good girl. I would often ask my dad if he would paint the bedroom but he never got round to it.

Malcolm didn't ask me to play his game for a few weeks after this but eventually we found ourselves back in that room again, me and my sister masturbating him, but he didn't physically touch me. He would often remind me about the consequences of telling tales and how much trouble I would be in.

I honestly thought that I was naughty and wrong for what happened and the devil's face on my bedroom ceiling was waiting to get me if I said anything. The damp patch on the ceiling became so life like, its eyes moved and watched over me and I could even see its face moving, turning from side to side watching every move that I made.

My dad used to take all seven kids to the swimming baths every Sunday, whist my mum stayed at home and made a roast dinner. We were never allowed any drinks or snacks and I remember how hungry I used to feel. I could smell the roast dinner as we walked towards our flat and remember the feeling of hunger and how I couldn't wait to eat it my dinner. I devoured my dinner so quickly, my plate was clean within minutes, my stomach rumbled so loudly you would think I hadn't eaten in weeks, but actually I had my breakfast in the morning. I can understand now why my dad wouldn't let us eat anything after swimming, the hard work my mum put into making a meal for so many people was appreciated by all.

My mum always bought two tins of Heinz puddings and made steaming hot custard for afters. We only had a small portion because it was shared out between seven of us. I would always put my finger in the tin to try and scrape out any bits that were stuck on the sides.

But even these memories were darkened. When we went to the swimming baths, Malcolm used to push my head deep down into the water using my hair and would only let me up when I was gasping for breath, just as I took one deep breath he would push me under the water again and keep repeating this.

Looking back at this I think he was trying to drown me, the experience was so intense and not in any way fun. Sometimes I went crying to my dad and he would tell Malcolm off for being so rough. Malcolm would defend this by saying I was being a baby and he was only playing. He wasn't playing; I swear he was hoping that I would drown so his dirty little secret wouldn't come out.

Not long after Malcolm raped me, it was bonfire night and my sister and I decided to make a Guy Fawkes so we could ask people for money, "Penny for the guy?" We spent weeks making this and kept it hidden at the side of my sisters' bed. My mum and dad would not allow us to go out with the Guy Fawkes as they thought it was dangerous asking strangers for money.

Sometimes, we were allowed to play outside the flat door when it was dark, there were two other flats facing ours on the landing. Some teenagers would get hold of some fireworks and let them off outside on the landing near our flat door. It was so much fun, one of the fireworks was called a rip-rack, once lit, it would zigzag on the floor and I would run in laughter trying to avoid it hitting my legs, quite dangerous really but that is how it was back then.

One night, we were allowed to stay up late, probably around 10 pm. Malcolm decided to play a prank, he had hidden at the side of my sister's bed and pretended to be the Guy Fawkes, making out that it had come to life. He spoke the threatening words again “Keep your mouth shut!” I thought it was for real and the Guy Fawkes had come to life and thought this must be linked to the Devil’s face on the damp bedroom ceiling. Then Malcolm let out a giggle, he thought this was hilarious scaring two little girls. He had a sick sense of humour and certainly got pleasure out of making constant reminders for us to keep quite.

Around Christmas time, my mum, dad, auntie and uncle went to a party in a flat a few floors above our flat, my brothers were babysitting us. I think all the adults were fairly drunk.

Later on my mum and dad came home, my auntie went back to her home and my uncle stayed at the party. I could hear people talking and the noise of this woke me up, I got out of bed and walked into the lounge.

My older brother Tim ran into the room and told my dad that my uncle had fallen down the concrete stairs and was out cold. I followed my dad out of the flat and there was my uncle lying on the floor lifeless. My dad called an ambulance.

My uncle was in hospital for a couple of months, he had brain damage from falling down the stairs drunk. I have a lot of aunties and uncles but these two were my favourites and I often played with my cousins which are their children. They had seven children, just like our family and my auntie must not have been coping too well with my uncle being in hospital.

Before long all of them stayed at our flat for nearly two months, my aunt and my seven cousins. We were overcrowded as it was and it just became chaotic with so many more people, I don't know how my mum and dad managed this but they certainly gave my auntie the support she needed.

The first couple of days were madness but I noticed my brother could not make us play his game. I felt safe, knowing that he would not get the chance to hurt me.

A few weeks went by, it was Sunday evening "bath night", my mum put all us three small kids in the bath and washed our hair, she didn't half rub our scalps and the way my mum washed me hair always hurt. We always had a quick bath because there was usually someone else waiting to use the toilet or to have a bath. My mum got my brother and sister out first and I asked if I could stay in the water for a bit longer to play.

Eventually the water started to get cold and I shouted out at my mum, "Can you get me out now I'm cold?" The bathroom door was slightly open and then Malcolm came in, he shouted to my mum, "I'll get her dried, I need the toilet." He locked the door behind him before turning and picking me up out of the water.

He put me down on a wet towel, he had another towel in his hand and started to dry me. He kept rubbing me in between my legs with the towel and he started to hurt my skin. He dropped the towel and continued rubbing me with his hand. He pushed me on to the floor, "Keep your mouth shut!" He pulled his pants down and forced his penis inside me. It hurt so much, such a burning sensation which caused my little body to tremble.

A minute later someone was trying to open the bathroom door. He pulled his pants up and said, "Just a minute." He wrapped a towel around me and grabbed my arm tightly causing my skin to welt and bruise; he whispered menacingly, "Keep your fucking trap shut!"

He opened the bathroom door and my mum was walking towards us, Malcolm told her that I wouldn't get out the bath and I was messing about. I got told off for being naughty because there were other people waiting for a bath. She ordered me to go to my bedroom to get dressed so nobody could see me. I could not understand why I had a telling off, it was my brother's fault and not mine.

I think his games came to a stop not long after Christmas and didn't happen again, but the memories were still there. My auntie went back home when my uncle was discharged from hospital.

My childhood soon became miserable, I always seemed to have a knot in my stomach, always on edge that I would get found out for the horrible things that I had done, I didn't want or like to get into trouble.

I feared Malcolm's constant reminders, threats and the devil that he put in my bedroom to watch over me. This was the last thing I saw at night and the first thing I saw in the morning. The face on the wall was waiting for me to crumble and tell, it was ready to reach out and hurt me.

I have mixed thoughts on my age when this started happening, but looking back I was a lot younger than eight. The memories I have are still somewhat confusing regarding my age and this is because I have put what happened away for so many years out of pure fear. I must have blocked out what had happened.

I didn't and couldn't tell anyone of what has happened. As months went by, I became somewhat of a rebel and looked for ways where I would get into trouble and get caught and punished. I would let tyres down on cars and play knock a door run, go to places that I wasn't allowed and sometimes I would help myself to my dad's spirits, gagging with every mouthful.

As time started passing, my family began to get older and before long we all became adults. I had become so good at burying the truth that I didn't remember him raping me.

It sounds impossible that I could forget but I had spent so long burying it and my life had taken such a turn that I had become a changed person, although I have always remembered the days he made my sister and I masturbate him.

Those memories never failed, possibly because it was such a frequent occurrence. The memory of this was like an awful nightmare that I doubted could have happened, but on the rare occasions I have brought this up in conversation with my sister she would confirm that the nightmare was indeed real. I suppose this is something that I could not face and decided to block these awful thoughts out as they felt so distant.

I have always remained fairly close to my family as we turned into adults, including my brother Malcolm. I suppose we had a kind of normal relationship that any brother/sister would have, he got married and eventually so did I. He often visited me and my husband, sometimes for a few hours at a time and we used to laugh and joke like nothing had happened and everything was so normal.

I would often look at him and think he must have forgotten what he did to me, or he thought I was too young to remember anything, or is it just ignorance? For whatever reason, I have never seemed to have quite balanced this out.

I didn't hate Malcolm; I think I just buried my thoughts, unable to think of this as a reality and all seemed like a haze. Looking back, the rape must have been too much for me to absorb at such a young age. The horror was a part of my life that I was unable to face.

I can now clearly remember in detail what happened as these images have really come clear in my memories. I may have some of the wording wrong on what was actually said, but the accounts given of these horrible times are as real now as they were then. My recognition to my actual age when all this started happening still remains uncertain. I know the incident with the bath was at an age where I needed help getting in/out of the bath.

My brother Malcolm had plenty of friends and I get the feeling that he and one his friends had forced themselves on other girls as their threats and traits seem similar. They both told me to keep quiet and the words and actions resulted in the same outcomes, which you will understand my thinking on this as we go into the next chapter of my shameful past.

## *Chapter 2*

### *A ten year old girl*

My four older brothers seemed to have the same network of friends, about twenty of them used to knock around together and I knew most of them as they were regular faces in my life. I sometimes played football with them on the football pitch behind the flats in Kersal. Very often the Manchester United team used to practice here, Georgie Best and Bobby Chalton would have a kick around with us kids, kicking the ball to one and another above our heads. It was like piggy in the middle, all I knew was that they had nicked our ball and wouldn't give it back.I remember pointing out Georgie Best to my dad when he was watching the match on TV, "Dad that's the man who keeps nicking my ball!" I didn't know they were famous at the time; I was too young to recognise this. My family were all Man United fans.

Funny really when I look back on this, the rules and mentality with professional football has changed so much over the years and this certainly wouldn't happen now.

My brothers and their mates would often join us when we played British Bulldog, apart from my oldest brother Tim. Malcolm was always in the loop, I just treated him as normal although I was scared of him and avoided him as much as I could.

It wasn't always bad with Malcolm and sometimes he would be nice to me and be a normal brother, like my other brothers. There were often other times he would just glare at me as a reminder to keep quite. I would always be nervous around him in case he turned on me again.

Back then, the summer days were very hot and you could recognise each season with changes in weather. Winter was always thick snow, there was always a foggy period, a period where all the leaves fell of the trees and a period when all the daffodils came out.

As a child, I loved it when it was snowing, especially when it had frozen over. There is a really steep road where Salford University is now. Back then, virtually every kid on the block made up their own make shift snow sledges. We would go right to the top of the road and whizz back down on our sledges, more often than not the sledge would tip over. The hill was so steep and slippery; I found it hard to stand up without slipping back down.

Days like this were so much fun and daring; fairly often I would graze my knees by trying to do some dare devil stunt. I would carry on playing and was having too much fun to cry over the grazes I had.

When I got too cold, I would run back home and get warm in front of the fire, my clothes were always wet and cold. I would get changed and would end up putting socks on my hands because my gloves were wet. My mum would try to get me to stay in because I got so cold. This didn't bother me; I just want to have fun with everyone else.

On one summers day when I was around 10 years old, I was walking back home from my auntie's who lived a few minutes' walk from my home, this was during the summer holidays from school. I had only been allowed to go there on my own for a couple of months and really enjoyed playing with my cousins.

It was still daylight when I started to walk home and I had to be home for a certain time, I think this was for 4.30 pm although I would be guessing this. Not long after leaving my auntie's, one of my brother's friends Ben shouted me and ran towards me to catch up.

It was a really hot summer's day and I had to shield my eyes from the blazing son, putting my hand above my eyebrows so I could see who he was.

Ben asked me if I wanted to play tag with him, he was probably 17 years old and often joined in when we played British Bulldog so I didn't find his request strange. He was a familiar face and knocked around with my brothers. I told him I couldn't play because I would be late home and would get into trouble.

Nearly all the teenagers tormented us little kids when we played with them, not in a nasty way, it just must of been one of those things back them.

Ben decided to play tag with me anyway regardless of what I said and kept poking and prodding me saying, "Tag, you're it!"

I didn't want to play and he kept prodding trying to get me to join in and play. He prodded and prodded me and pushed me towards some garages on the opposite side from the road where my auntie lived, her house was still visible. He wouldn't give up and was still trying to coax me into playing.

The garages had gaps at the side of them with overgrown grass and bushes, behind the garages sat the River Irwell. Opposite the garages were rows of houses and there were people walking down the street, some cutting down privet bushes in their gardens.

He continued to prod and push me in a playful way until we ended up in between the recesses at garages. I kept telling him to let me pass and that my mum would go mad at me for being late. He wouldn't let me get passed him. I got really scared because of how overpowering he had become.

He started play fighting and wrestled me to the floor; my brother Malcolm came to mind at this point. My face was pushed down into some nettles on the floor, my skin was really hurting as my head was moved from side to side and seemed like he knew that the nettles were hurting me.

There were shrivelled weeds and rubbish that people had dumped there and it seemed so dirty and dismal. He carried on play fighting but became really rough and said all he wanted to do was play with me and told me to stop being a spoil sport.

He started to pull my knickers down, the top of my legs were burning because of how rough he was and then he pulled them of completely. It felt like he had ripped the skin off the top of my legs as I tried to stop him.

I know that I was crying at this point because my legs were really hurting, he was so strong and made me feel powerless to fight back. I remember thinking he was going to kill me and I sort of went limp and felt so weak like all my strength had left my body because I had been struggling futilely to get away. My cry meant nothing to him and he carried on regardless.

He turned me over on my back and pinned my arms over my head with one hand, I started screaming at him, "Get off me! Get off me!" I must have been making too much noise because he covered my mouth and nose with his hand.

He was sweating and I felt his drips of sweat land on my cheek, he just kept saying "Shush, Shush. Be quiet!"

The grip he had on my nose and mouth began to tighten and I thought I was going to die. I tried to bite my way through his hand and he eventually took his hand away.

He kept asking me if I was ticklish with a playful tone to his voice and he started to tickle me under my arms and then down below. I think I was sort of prepared for what was coming and it was the reason why I felt limp, it was like being back with my brother. I had the same horrible sickly feeling and sensed that he was going to do what my brother had done.

He kept flipping me over like a rag doll, from my back, to my side and onto my front. My skin was hurting almost everywhere from the nettles I was lying on.

I felt something hard pressing against my bottom. He kept telling me to keep still and he wouldn't let me go as he struggled to put his penis inside me. At first he miscalculated causing me so much pain. I honestly felt that I was going to snap in half through his weight and his roughness, at the time I almost wished that I did snap in half as being dead would have been a more positive experience for me.

He must have realised that he misdirected as I screamed out in pain. He put his hand over my mouth and in a gentle voice said he was sorry for hurting me and he'd let me go if I kept quiet.

I kept trying to get away from him but his strength was so mighty. He just kept me there eventually putting his penis where he had intended. He kept repeating himself, telling me with such a gentle tone to his voice, "Shush and keep still." It was almost like he was trying to reassure and comfort me.

He pulled me so close to him and kept stopping for very short periods, he sort of kissed and licked my cheek and kept saying shush!

His penis kept slipping out and he would put it back in regardless of where he put it. The pain was worsening and I really thought he would kill me if I dared shout out again.

I will never forget the smell of his bad breath, his overwhelming body odour and the drips of sweat that hit my little screwed up face.

I felt like I was going to split in half. He had broken my tiny body but carried on regardless, putting his penis in wherever it would fit. Every entry from him hurt but one lot of pain was worse than the other. I wanted to die and end this excruciating pain, but had to perceiver until he stopped.

Eventually the pain lessened, he must have satisfied himself. He reverted back to tickling me under the arms and kept repeating, “Are you ticklish? We’re just playing.”

Finally, he let me get up. I was sobbing. He stopped me in my tracks when I tried to run away from him, grabbing my arm he told me I couldn’t go yet. He tried to comfort me by hugging and putting his fingers through my hair and whispering “Awe, don’t cry. I won’t hurt you, shush, shush!” He looked like a giant compared to my height.

He asked me if I was going to tell anyone. I remember screaming at him in a hysterical voice, “My brothers are going to beat you up, they’re going to get you.”

He gripped my arm tightly then dragged me to the River Irwell. The stench of the river was vile and debris of branches, carrier bags and other things were floating on top of the water. He pushed me in.

The water was so cold and dirty, I held on for dear life to the long grass on the bank of the river. He crouched down near me and started laughing, “Tell me you’re going to keep quiet, do you really want to drown and get eaten by worms?” He prized my hands open and forced me to let go of the long grass I was so desperately clinging on to and the only thing stopping me from slipping away into the cold dark river.

It was as though he wanted me to float away and drown; although I did think at this point drowning would have been an escape for me. I have heard people saying that there were rats in the river, would they have eaten me?

As I splashed in the water looking for a way back to safety, he turned and walked away, leaving me there alone in the rancid water.

Petrified, I had no choice but to at least try and save myself. It took all my might but I scrambled my way to the river bank before trying to pull myself out of the water using the long grass as a rope. I kept slipping back in the water because the bank was wet and the mud was slippery, eventually I got on solid ground.

For a few minutes I was too scared to walk, expecting him to peer around the corner and push me in again. Eventually I got the courage and prised myself up before walking over to the end of the garage wall, slowly peering my head around the corner to make sure that he had gone.

I started to make my way home; nobody stopped or looked at me, not one person. A little girl, clearly shaken, wet, full of mud and walking away from the garages and river didn't catch anyone's eye, people just carried on as normal. I just can't understand, there were plenty of people that must have seen something and nobody battered an eyelid.

I didn't have any knickers on and the inside of my legs at the top were all chaffed. I tried to run but could barely walk with the pain. I thought I had wet myself.

My legs were like jelly and remember thinking I was going to get into trouble for being late home.

As I started to walk to my front door, I was overwhelmed as the feeling of safe wafted over me. I walked in and I saw my mum's face, such a comfort. She took one look at me and uttered, "Look at the state of you!" I looked down, my clothes and legs were all muddy and I broke down in tears, sobbing I told mum and dad that a bad man had thrown me into the river.

My brother Malcolm appeared. His presence stopped me in my tracks; I couldn't reveal what had really happened. The look he was giving me with his piercing eyes terrified me; I didn't dare say what else had really gone on.

I thought Malcolm was a part of it and he had somehow set it up. Those words crept into my mind again, those five little words that kept a control of me. Even though no words were said, in my head the words were clear, "Keep your fucking mouth shut!"

My little heart was pounding and my mind flickered to the devil's face on my bedroom ceiling.

I was still at an age where I didn't know what sex was, what a penis was or what rape was. This was at an age where I was still in primary school; I recall it happening at the end of the school holidays as the week after I went back at school.

I know the Police were called out and I was questioned by two of them, my mum was sat by my side and the police gave me mug shots to look at. As I sat looking, all I could see was strangers. I of course knew who he was, but was too afraid to tell so did not identify anyone.

I don't remember what happened with the police after this and never wanted to ask.

The next day I was bleeding and very sore, the inside of my legs at the top were red raw and felt bruised. My body was broken and I felt like I was going to be sick.

I told my mum that I was bleeding a bit and got told that I must have started my periods. I didn't even know what a period was and still didn't know that I had been raped, just that I was hurt. I could barely go to the toilet I was that sore, but how could I ask my mum to make me better without my brother finding out? How could I tell anyone with the hold my brother had over me and how could she not know what had happened to me?

I hated going to bed at night, the vision of the devil was so real, his face had become clearer and I would look and stare at this every night, a constant reminder to keep quiet, I'm in the wrong, it's my fault. I dreaded going to sleep because I thought he would take me away, my eyes would feel heavier and heavier as I tried to fight going to sleep.

## *Chapter 3*

## *Friend's death*

Months later I went to the park with my friend Josh. I was allowed to go to the park because there were plenty of adults around and there was always one of my brothers there or nearby.

Josh was on his little scooter, scooting by the swings as other kids was swinging on them. Normally we would both go on the swings, seesaw, slide or roundabout or wait for our turn if other kids were on.

On this particular day, my brother and his friends turned up at the park. I remember panicking and thinking that it was someone else's turn to hurt me, that's why they were there at the park. They all looked as big as grownups, too big for a children's park.

I clearly remember saying to Josh, "Hurry up or they will get us." As I said these words, my friend Josh turned around to look at them.

Being too young to recognise the dangers, a wooden swing caught him under the neck and sent him hurtling into the air. It all seemed like it was in slow motion, his face seemed fearless and he eventually came hurtling to the ground. The sound when his tiny body impacted the concrete floor will remain with me for life.

His body sprawled over the floor, his ear and nose were bloody and he had white foam coming out of his mouth, he was making gurgling sounds. I felt sick. I didn't know what the white foam was but it reminded me of the Darlics on TV.

Some teenagers picked his tiny body up off the concrete floor and put him on the grass. I suppose they put him on the grass so that he was more comfortable but would he have survived if he was left until the ambulance came? The answer I will never know.

I remember someone telling me to run to his house and tell his mum he was unconscious. My little legs couldn't go any faster and it seemed like I was running for hours before I eventually got there, my heart was beating so fast and kept trying to get my breath and then I couldn't remember how to pronounce the word "unconscious". So I just grabbed her hand and kept telling her to hurry.

The ambulance was there when I got back to the park and I couldn't get anywhere near Josh. I could see the blood stains on the concrete floor and picture the white foam coming out of his mouth. The ambulance took him away. Later that day he died.

If I had not been so scared he would not have ran in

front of the swing, my fear resulted in his death. I have always blamed myself for his death; it was me that distracted him because of my fear of my brother and his friends, I will always bear the scars of this.

This tragic end to Josh's life became another part of the devil's face. It was like the face was laughing and became more profound each time something bad happened.

I know now that the face that I described as the devil was my imagination, but at the time it was so real and I believed that it was watching me.

A few years later my family moved to a different area, not because of anything that had happened, we just moved on in life I suppose.

## *Chapter 4*

## *The Sadist*

My family moved to Cheshire when I was 12 years old and I was in the second year of high school. We moved into a three story townhouse with five bedrooms. The house had been newly built and was like a mansion compared to the flat, it smelt so new. I remember how excited I was when we got the keys; I went into every room and cupboard exploring our new home.

My sister and I were the first ones to choose a bedroom; we chose the only one which had a sink in it. The room was very large compared to the one that we had.

We had to be quick and put some of our stuff in the bedroom before someone else claimed 'dibs' on it. I think all of my family were excited about the move, it was like we had moved into a posh area compared to the built up tower blocks in Kersal.

Before long I started a new high school and met new friends and was fairly happy. Nevertheless I really missed my other true friends from Salford, here people my age seemed to have different dress codes and had fake personalities. My impression was that they were stuck up and not real people.

I was somewhat of a tom boy and used to wear baseball boots and skinners, always prepared to have a fight or pick a fight with someone. Yet my new friends wore tights and make up, it reminded me of the Stepford wives as they had to look perfect, to me they were strange and weird. Their idea of fun was putting make up on, this was certainly was not what I was about.

This made me feel uncomfortable but I did not let it change my character or dress. I suppose looking back on this I felt that I had to be on the defensive and keep my guard up whilst in the presence of these strange people.

I wore my baseball boots when I first started the new high school, as I normally would. This created trouble for me from day one and I got into some fights with kids my age and others who were older than me. People would say, "Do you think you are hard wearing those?" My reply would often be, "Why do you want me to put my foot in your mouth and find out?" Some would back off, and others wanted to put me in my place, especially the girls in the year above me.

I would never back down and always stood my ground and actually looked forward to having a fight, I was no bully but certainly would not let anyone get the better of me.

I did make some good friends and had plenty of laughs, got into trouble like most teenagers and didn't give my past a second thought. I became a rebel, fearing nothing.

I did miss the normal friends that I grew up with from Salford. These were salt of the earth and didn't put on any hairs and graces. What you saw is what you got!

As I started my teenage life I had plenty of boyfriends like most girls but could never commit to any relationship. When it came to the stage where I kissed a boy I would finish with them within a few days. Some boys tried it on and I suppose this was normal for teenage lads. I had no interest in experimenting or giving anyone the opportunity to have sex with me. I would feel like I was being overpowered if they tried to get personal and ended up ditching them for this reason.

I didn't think of my past during most of my teenage years as I must off chose not to remember, although sometimes I would have flashbacks which I could never make sense off.

At one point I thought there was something different about me, my friend's seemed to keep the same boyfriend for months and some even had sex and bragged about it. I had no desire to follow suit and didn't want what they wanted, I just wanted fun with my friends.

I have always felt that something was missing in my life and that I was incomplete, I couldn't really say how, just that something was not quite right.

Being a teenager, I liked to keep up with the fashion in my tom boyish style. My mum and dad used to go into their local pub and when they got back, I would fleece my dad for money when he had a few to drink, I would say that I needed a new dress, shoes etc and asked him to promise me that he would give me a hundred quid the next day. By the next day he would have forgot about the promise and say to my mum, "Why didn't you stop me?" This is quite funny as my dad would never break a promise and I knew that and this is why I always asked when he was fairly drunk. I had my dad wrapped around my little finger but always appreciated what I got.

When I was around fifteen years old, I would ask my dad for some pocket money to meet my friends in the town centre. We used to go to town on a weekly basis and have lunch at the Co-op before shopping for new clothes.

There was always a few of us that met up and we had some good laughs and quite often got into some sort of bother. These are the good memories and I often reflect back on them.

On one particular Saturday, one of my friends started chatting to some lad she had met and was desperate to date him. We had seen him before in town occasionally and she really fancied him. He didn't really show any interest in her, but he seemed a friendly sort of person and I could see why she was attracted to him.

His mate Dan made it obvious that he liked me and started chatting to me, he seemed okay but I had no interest in going out with him as he was not my type. Nonetheless, my friend talked me round into going out with him on a double date so that she could try to get a date with his friend.

I didn't like or fancy Dan, especially not enough to even consider any form of relationship with him. I suppose me being me, I didn't want to let my friend down so I ended up going along with this for my friend's sake. To me this meant that I would see Dan maybe once or the maximum of twice then I would put an end to it.

This did not go to plan as I couldn't get shut of Dan, he just wouldn't take the hint and in all honesty I could not have been any blunter with him. I made it so obvious that I had no interest and that we are finished. Usually this is a straight forward thing to do. I didn't act like his girlfriend and just treated him like a friend. He was like a sort of friend that everyone just wanted to avoid, including me.

Dan and I were still 'seeing each' other for a couple of months, even at this point I still had no interest in him, I just couldn't get rid of him regardless of what measures I put in place. It was like we were kind of friends, or I should say he felt I was his friend and I thought he just liked hanging around with us.

For some reason he presumed we were an item, I certainly did not in any way lead him on to believe this as I had no interest what so ever in him. I just hadn't found the way to get rid of him gently, whatever I tried he dissuaded and he dissolved any intention I had.

There were a few kisses from him and I reacted to his kisses with a quick peck back, he certainly made it hard work for me to finish our so called relationship. I don't really know why I kissed him back even if the kisses were a quick peck. I suppose the pressure from him and the fact that me being too nice of a person prevented me to actually say the words that I didn't like him? It was like he knew that I didn't like him and he was always prepared to boycott the situation of me finishing with him.

He tried to get more personal with, I made it clear that I had no interest and rejected him. He was so difficult to get rid of and I guess that I was hoping he would just fade away and would get the hint, but this did not happen.

Within the first two months he seemed to know where I was or where I was going all the time and turned up.

Looking back I know now that he must have been stalking me and watching my home because he wouldn't have known where I was, or what my plans would be otherwise.

My main problem was me as I hate hurting someone's feelings. I was too nice to just come out and say I didn't like him. Still showing no interest in him, he treated me like I was his girlfriend and I treated him like a friend I wanted to drop. He was always there like a bad penny and this started to annoy me.

I guess in the end I just put up with him being there, it was like he was very determined to be with me, I didn't hate him but didn't want any kind of relationship with him.

Looking back at this, I feel like I was groomed into this hideous relationship and he seemed to take control of me although I did not realise this at the time or recognise any signs.

He could be quite funny sometimes and had a weird sort of dominating personality. I could still not understand why would he want to be with me when I made it obvious I had no interest in him? He kept telling me how beautiful I was and how lucky he was to be with me.

He would turn up everywhere I went and he was never invited. He would appear from nowhere, even when I went to the local bus stop to go to town.

By my 16th birthday this charade had been going on nearly three months. He took it upon himself to organise a party at his house to celebrate my birthday. He invited quite a lot of people, more of his friends were present and I hardly knew any of them, there were only a few of my friends there. I was only told by him on the day of the party and he said he planned it as a surprise for me and told me I was worth every bit of effort. Being polite and not wanting to sound ungrateful, I went along with it.

Deep down, I hated the thought of what he had done and this is not how I wanted to celebrate my sixteenth birthday. My plan was to go out with my friends and having a good laugh and certainly not a party at his home. He put me in a position where I felt I couldn't get out of it without upsetting a lot of people, so I had to except what he had done.

He had bought lots of booze for the occasion, not really the ideal thing for a sixteen year old girl. He was twenty one and his mates ranged from this age to approximately thirty year olds. I felt very uncomfortable and this was not my sort of thing and I actually felt out of place, like a kid with a bunch of grownups. I couldn't understand why his mates were at a 16th birthday party, they looked so old and I didn't know any of them.

I did not know enough about Dan and had only known him for a short period of time. He really had no right to organise this, but as he said he wanted to surprise me and he had made a lot of effort to make my 16th a birthday I would never forget.

I was stood up in the kitchen talking with my friends and felt like Dan was listening to every word I said, he kept pestering me to have a drink, "It's your 16th birthday, you should be getting hammered." I made myself juice instead, my dad would have gone ape with me if he found I had been drinking alcohol, and drinking did not appeal to me and especially under the circumstances.

It was all too much for me and I found the atmosphere quite overwhelming, especially because of the age of some of his friends and the way some of them were looking at me. I didn't feel comfortable being there and kept trying to think of reasons on how I could get out of it.

An hour or two went by and others seemed fairly drunk and having a good time. The music was blasting; I was surprised his neighbours did not complain.

Dan kept trying to kiss me, eventually & reluctantly I kissed him back in the hope of appeasing him so he'd leave me alone. His breath smelt of stale booze and the kiss was very short without any passion. I kissed him back briefly out of guilt but the way I scrunched up my face should have given him the hint that I wasn't interested.

He wrapped his arms around my back and gripped me firmly as he tried to kiss me again. I tried to pull away from him but before I knew it he had backed me into a bedroom. He closed the door behind him and pushed me onto the bed, stumbling on top of me. He tried to kiss me again and put his hand on my bust. I made it clear that I didn't want this; I kept desperately trying to push him off me.

When I knew what his intentions were I told him, "No way is this happening, not a chance!" I kept trying to get up and leave the room. His strength overpowered my weakness and I couldn't get him off me. He kept me pinned down and raped me.

Throughout I continued to struggle and repeatedly told him to get off. His hands were holding my wrists tightly and pushed them into the mattress. His strength and will overpowered any attempt of me escaping. He totally ignored my attempt to make him stop and just carried on.

I took my mind to a different place to block out what he was doing as I eventually accepted that I had to go through with it. It was like an outer body experience, I felt that I was there but it wasn't happening to me. I know that I did not lead him on in any way to do this, nor did I consent once.

The smell of stale ale on his breath was horrible; he had a lot to drink and was drunk. He kept me pinned down for around fifteen minutes; I froze, I couldn't scream or shout out, I just froze. My mind took me back to my childhood, not the rapes as these memories were well hidden and buried deep in a 'Pandora's Box' in my memory. I focused on that damp patch on my bedroom ceiling, the 'devil's face' from my childhood coming back as a reminder to keep quiet.

After he had finished he told me how fantastic I was and how lucky he was to have me, I felt so flat and emotionless.

I come out the bedroom and just carried on with the party in a fashion, feeling lost and out of place. I remember thinking it wasn't really me that was there, it was like I was in a daze, in a world of my own. I had an overwhelming feeling of hopelessness and defeat. I didn't know what else to do apart from keep quiet and yet in my head I was screaming at everyone, "Please help me!"

Nobody was listening to me; people were laughing and talking like I didn't exist. Their voices seemed like miles away and not one person noticed what Dan had done.

I must have been shaking as one of my friends commented on it. I just felt horrible and thought it was my fault so did nothing nor said anything, after all I must have asked it!

About an hour later he came over to me and held me by the hand, then led me away from others. He guided my head up using his hands until we made eye contact; he had tears in his eyes. He gave a poor excuse of an apology, telling me that he loved me so much and that he couldn't resist.

He made out that he had the right to do this as he 'had waited and been patient with me for months'. He had the nerve to tell me that I was worth the wait. I did not reply to this as I still felt numb and that it wasn't me that was there, it was like I was watching and listening through somebody else's body. The experience is so hard to explain, why didn't I do anything, why did I just accept what had happened?

Dan placed a drink of orange juice in my hand and asked if I was okay and then stood back watching me like a hawk. When he caught my eye he just smiled at me like he thought everything was happy and acceptable.

After some time people started to leave the party and go home, some were fairly drunk. The air was thick with the stench of stale ale and it was knocking me sick, I started to feel strange and light headed.

One of my friends asked me if I was walking home with her, Dan replied on my behalf and told her that he was going to walk me home in a few minutes. I think I was in shock and didn't comment or really catch on to this properly. I just noticed that hardly anyone was left.

I felt relieved as I thought everyone had been watching me knowing what I had done.

The shame I felt was immense, my head numb and cold, I held my head down in denial and my body still shaking.

I went to stand up from my seat, my whole body felt weird; my legs were like jelly and wouldn't hold my weight. I had trouble trying to focus and could feel my arms floating; this feeling took over the rest of my body. Looking back now I know he spiked my orange juice.

I can't really remember too much after this apart from Dan asking me if I was okay, his voice sounded like he was talking in slow motion and then he stood next to me holding me up. My body felt like it didn't have any weight to it and felt like I was floating.

Suddenly I felt the sensation of moving, like I was being pulled and my feet were dragging on the floor. The room was spinning in a warped sort of way and I couldn't focus on anything but this. We must have made it to the bedroom because I became aware that I was being tied to the bed by both my arms and legs. I didn't know what was happening to me, my whole body felt like a feather and I could hear muffled voices like people were underwater trying to talk.

I could feel the presence of someone being on top of me and I had no control over my body. I felt that I was floating and seemed to be in a dreamy sort of state. I couldn't make out the features on the face as it looked distorted and out of shape and when the person spoke their lips seemed gigantic and their voice was so weird, I couldn't understand any of the words.

I had no weight to my body and was powerless to have any kind of reaction. I can remember some of the things that were happening to me but felt neither pain nor emotion. It could have been more than one person for all I know; deep down I know there was more than one. I don't know to the full extent what they did to me, what I do remember is disgusting and shameful.

The whole experience of this is still like a haze, my whole body felt like a feather but also felt like led. It was like I was awake but not aware and couldn't seem to move, it seemed like it was some sort of a dream but was in fact a hazy nightmare.

I can't even remember who he or they were, but I do know this happened and I have a fairly good idea of what they did to me, other parts are still very hazy and maybe this should be left like this.

I think it was a few hours later when I was untied, my arms and legs felt like dead weight and I struggled to stay sat up.

I must have left at some point but cannot remember leaving. I just seemed to find myself walking home on my own; clueless to what time and day it was apart from it being very dark. I know I found it hard to coordinate my movements, I wanted to run but my legs felt so heavy and felt that I wasn't moving forward with each step I took.

People passed by me and stared at me like I was so kind of a drunk or druggie, I felt that I was in some sort of dream and everything was in slow motion.

As I reached my home, I had the feeling of dread because of how late it was, although I didn't have a clue of what hour it was but I knew I would be in a lot of trouble.

As I walked through the door, my dad was raging at me and said he had been looking everywhere for me and he was ready to call the police. He took his belt from his pants and repeatedly asked me where I had been and who with before using his belt to hit me.

I have never seen my dad so worked up and I got a right old pasting. I didn't feel any of this; it was like I was immune from pain. My mouth kept drooling and I couldn't control this.I couldn't tell him what had happened, nor collate the words together to attempt giving any explanation. I felt so dirty and ashamed and was in disbelief of what I had done.

I didn't have any shoes on when I got home and still no one asked me if I was okay. I was made to feel like a cheap worthless tart.

My dad just presumed that I was drunk but the truth is I didn't have any alcohol that I was aware of or had knowingly consumed. I think if I did try and tell him he would have turned a deaf ear to it because of how angry he was. He told me to get out of his sight and I had to go straight to bed and said he will deal with me in the morning.

The next morning, my dad had a go at me and told me I should be ashamed of myself for coming home in such a state and that I was a disgrace for getting drunk and coming in so late.

He threatened me and told me in no uncertain terms that if I ever came home again in that state again he would take his belt of to me again. He looked so disappointed in me which made me feel a whole lot worse, like I had let him down.

I couldn't tell anyone the truth of what had happened, it must have been my fault, I must have asked for this to happen. I remember thinking what a slut I was, my skin felt like it was crawling and I could smell sex all over me.

First thing I did after my dad's lecture is put loads of bleach in the bath and as much soap as I could get my hands on. The water felt like it was scalding, the hotter it was, the more chance I would have of killing all the germs and washing away handprints or whatever else was on me and inside me. I lay there thinking that nobody loved or cared about me, I just felt so alone, isolated and so messed up.

I began to scrub myself with a stiff nail brush, I felt so dirty and ashamed. I just sobbed and sobbed uncontrollably but there was nobody to put their arms around me and tell me everything was going to be all right.

When I got out of the bath I had marks all over my body from the scrubbing, some parts of my body were bleeding where I had scrubbed some of my skin away. Try as I might, I couldn't wash off the shame and filth. I had bruising in between my legs, on my hips, bottom and breast; I had love bites on most of these areas. Then I looked at the 'love and reassurance' that I had received from my dad in the form of welt marks across my legs and bottom from the belt he had used, my punishment for him being worried about me.

The following weeks I often picked up a razor blade and tried cutting my wrist, I really wanted to end my disgusting presence. Thinking about ending your life and actually seeing it through is not easy, each time I put the blade to my wrist I could not find the courage to go through with it.

I didn't try this to get any attention as I had already had enough of that from my disgusting behaviour. I presumed that everyone thought I was disgusting and a horrible person like I thought of myself.

Maybe I wouldn't have had suicidal thoughts if my family had noticed me and recognised that there was something wrong, this lack of care or compassion really contributed to my suicidal thoughts.

My friends called for me a few times over the next few days and weeks but I made some excuse not to go out with them. A few weeks went by before I got the courage to go out of the house again. My friend asked if I would go into town with her to do some shopping. I reluctantly went with her; I felt so edgy about going out but had decided that I needed to try.

It was late in the morning on a Saturday when we arrived in the town centre so we decided to go straight into the fashion shops.

My guard began to drop as we both walked around the shops laughing, like a girly day out should be. I still didn't confide in anyone about what happened as I didn't want anyone judging me again. As we walked in and out of the first few shops I would put my head down in shame when any guy so much as looked at me.

We were looking at tops in one shop when Dan appeared from nowhere with a grin on his face. How had I forgotten that he watches my every move? He must have followed me from my home again. He was like a little lap dog waiting for me to throw a ball to him; I couldn't get rid of him and felt very intimidated and frightened.

He was full of apologies and had tears in his eyes yet again, “Please don’t finish with me, I love you so much.” He held my hand, his palm felt so sweaty and I pulled my hand away. How could he think an apology would automatically warrant forgiveness?

He tagged along with us like he hadn’t done anything bad and like everything was completely normal. I felt my head going numb and starting sweating with fear too scared to react in any way. I could feel the colour draining out of my face and told my friend I wasn’t feeling well so we made our excuses and caught the bus home, leaving Dan in the town centre.

From this point he continued to push and push and make sure he was a part of my life regardless. I could not get rid of him, nor tell anyone as I had started to develop a real fear of him.

He seemed to turn up everywhere I went, like he was stalking me and waiting for me to leave my home, he was always one step ahead of me. At one point I became so untrusting that I thought one of friends had been telling him in advance where I was going, I became so paranoid and my head was really messed up.

Even at this early stage I become frightened of him. He made me feel vulnerable and that he had an evil hold over me. I spiralled into a nightmare of a twisted relationship, he would not be put off and was determined for ‘us to happen’ and be together.

He really knew how to work me and get into my head, causing such horrible dreaded fear, any strength or courage I had before had vanished.

Before long he slowly isolated me away from friends and started to control each day of my life like he owned me. For the first few weeks, he bought me gifts and tried to act like a perfect gentleman and would always make comments such as, “We are perfect and made for each other.” I was scared of him, I didn’t have any like or feelings for him. I wanted him out of my life; in fact I wanted him dead! I just wanted to get rid of him and he just wouldn’t let this happen.I became so terrified of him, this crushing hold he had on me, and the control he had over me was unreal.

Although I had no memory of my childhood rape at this point, I clearly remember being told “Shut up and say nothing.” This was a mantra that I lived by now.

Dan had a scar on his cheek which he had got when he was a child from a dog that attacked him. The freakiest thing, the scar was in the shape of my first initial.

His face became hideous; it terrified me, just as the devil’s face on the ceiling did. The dark and evil face that I had hidden away for so long came back to reality. I was convinced that I was owned by the devil himself.

The perfect gentleman act soon changed and his true self came back to the surface. I tried to end our so called relationship; this is where the horror escalated. I feared him from the day of my 16th birthday and felt that I was put in a position where I had no choice but to carry on.

When I did pluck up the courage and attempt to end this insanity it made things worse. It was then when he told me that if he couldn't have me, then nobody could and if I tried this again he would kill me and expressed that I belong to him. The way he looked at me sent shivers down my spine and I knew he meant every word.

He really got inside my head and controlled every part of my physical and mental well-being. I believed that I could not approach anyone about this, not even my family.

This gruelling hold he had on me made me believe that the devil had sent him to punish me. The scar on his face dominated my thoughts and seemed like a constant reminder that I belong to him and there was no way out.

It got to a point that almost every day he had sex with me, no love making, just dirty horrible and disgusting sex. Sex that I had to pretend to enjoy or he would turn on me. It wasn't just regular sex, he would tie me to the bed and do all sorts of sexual things to me, and often he would make me do things to him and was always violent during any of this.

Frequently he'd push my head down to his penis using my hair as a lever and make me do oral sex. He would push my head harder, forcing his penis further down my throat until I gagged. He was only bothered about him getting pleasure and discarded my reaction.

One day he took his sick fantasies further, he had a knife in his hand and told me to lie down on the bed then put the knife to my face. He seemed to be excited and found great pleasure in doing this. He asked me if I was scared and then stated, "If you not, you should be." Of course I was scared, I was trembling and thought he was going to kill me. He slowly moved the blade down from my neck and then down to my bra leaving a small line of blood where he has dug the knife in.

He stopped and looked at me, then said "Promise me that no one else will ever see your body?" He had a horrible twisted look in his eyes and then smiled. He positioned his knife under my bra and fiercely cut through it and then asked me if I was turned on. He then forced himself on me.

Whilst using me for his pleasure he took the knife and began to cut parts of my body, not deep enough to kill but enough to show his dominance. I honestly believed he would slit my throat. I tried my best to picture myself somewhere else and to switch off like I wasn't there, this proved to be too difficult.

Sometimes I would be physically sick whilst having sex and got battered for this, he reminded me this was a turn off and I would have to say something that would stop the beating. I would tell him that I was sick because of how excited I was. I would say anything that he wanted to hear as a survival tool and dreaded to think what he would do to me if he found out the truth of the disgust I felt for him.

He would always ask me if I enjoyed it, I would paint a smile on my face and tell him what he wanted to hear and yet my true thought was that I need to kill myself to get away from him, there was no way out for me.

I would often use bleach as mouth wash and sometimes I would even swallow some.I used bleach on a regular basis when I bathed or had a shower, I just needed to get rid of his germs and smell and wanted to wash away my thoughts of how dirty he made me feel. There was no detergent strong enough to remove this, nothing worked and the dirt wouldn't wash away.

I admit, I often wanted to take my own life and it came to a point where I went as far as writing a letter to my family to say how sorry I was for the suicide I had planned. I collected lots of different tablets for the occasion as I needed the right pills to make this work.

I even stole a bottle of booze from my dad to wash the pills down with.

I planned when I would take them, I chose bedtime because nobody would have suspected and it would have been too late for my family to do anything by the time they found me in the morning. I did not plan this to seek attention, I never told anybody about my plan, I planned it out of desperation to end my pointless and meagre life and I was sure I wanted to die.

I prepared myself to do this because I didn't know of any other way I could deal with my life. I had two choices, the first being that I killed myself or the second was to wait until he killed me. I was so determined to go through with this and I actually think that to get the courage to end your own life is so difficult and desperate and not just a step for attention, I wanted this so much and at the time something snapped in my head and I knew I had to do this.

Then a thought came into my head that stopped me in my tracks. If I did take my own life, his threats of what he would do to my family if I ever tried to leave him ticked over in my thoughts, he would never let me escape in life or death.

He had a way of really getting deep into my head and made me believe that when he had threatened to burn down my family home with my family in it he meant it. I believed every word he said.

Every day I was at my wits end and forever thinking "What next, what can I do to prevent his next binge of evil?" I certainly did not want him to meet my family but he made sure he got his foot in the door.

Of course he was on his best behaviour and tried to impress my family with his lies. Most of my family did not like him as they probably saw straight through him. I sensed this from the offset and prayed he did not catch on to this as I was aware of what he was capable of doing. I talked my mum and dad round and virtually begged them to give him a chance; they did this for my sake and because they did not have a clue about his nature and what he was doing to me.

My parents' house was quite large so privacy wasn't an issue, as he soon found out and used to his advantage. I actually felt I had some control as I was protected in my own home and did not think for one moment he would do anything to me whilst my family were around. After all, I had five brothers and my sister living there; they wouldn't stand back and let anything happen to me, would they? So I plucked up the courage and for the second time I told him that it was over. There was not much he could do to me with so many of my family around?

We were alone in a room but all my family were in the house and I knew I could shout out if I needed to and my brothers would batter him once they found out.

This soon backfired on me, the way he looked at me was like a death stare and his evil eyes sent shudders down my spine. His face scrunched with anger and his eyebrows seemed to meet in the middle.I knew I had to prepare myself for what he was about to do. He absolutely battered me, punching me in my back and stomach continuously. He grabbed my hair and used this as a lever to knock my head into a wall.

My family were clueless to what he was doing; I was not in a position to shout out and I just had to take it.

Once he had finished using me as a punch bag, he used his controlling voice, and said "I belong to him for life," and he "Would kill me if I finished with him." Then he threatened to come back later to burn the house down with my family inside, telling me how he would get great pleasure watching them burning to death.

He even accused me of seeing someone else and threatened to cut my throat, imitating the action by putting his hand around my throat and using a finger from the other hand to draw a line on my neck. He pressed hard on my throat with his finger and then drew his line, "I am going to slice you from ear to ear."

He then demanded sex, becoming overly passionate with me, telling me that nobody could ever turn me on the way he did. I just agreed and had sex, I couldn't wait for him to finish as I felt that my ribs were broken, the pain was intense.  For weeks after I found it really painful to breath, my ribs and back were bruised.

Dan was very crafty and made sure that the scars from his violence could be covered so that others couldn't see them. As for the mental injuries nobody had noticed them before so why would they now? He was pretty handy with his beatings and knew exactly what he was doing and where to do the damage.

He always apologised afterwards and cried his fake tears, making out he was sincerely sorry and would never do this again. He said we were soul mates and was meant to be together forever, "Please forgive me," he would beg and beg me knowing that these words meant nothing. I had no choice but to 'forgive' the evil bastard. Each time I told him he was forgiven, the bile would rise in my throat. So I told him what he wanted to hear, said I was sorry and didn't know what I was thinking.

After a few months my dad told me he didn't want Dan in the house again and that he thought he was a 'dirty bastard'. He warned me not to see him anymore. Dan didn't do anything in particular that stood out, my dad could just see straight through him. I reluctantly agreed with my dad not to see him again and pretended that I had finished with him.

I knew I couldn't do this and had to tell Dan about my dad and what he said. Of course, this was my fault again and this led to another beating before he threatened to cut my dad's throat in front of me and do the same to the rest of my family.

Eventually he apologised again to me for the beating and shed those false tears, drops of water that flowed from his evil and empty darkened eyes. He agreed to avoid my parents' home for a while, but made it clear to me that I had to fix this and shouldn't let anyone say anything bad about him.

He asked me what I was playing at and what I had been saying to make them dislike him. Of course he blamed me. It was always the same; everything that he disliked or went wrong was my fault.

He was always sorry for the beatings and rapes, there were always tears from him, and he would always tell me that he wouldn't do it again. This became a daily ritual for him, every day he would beat and rape me and then go through the same process of apologies and tears.

From that point on I had to meet him in secret so my dad didn't find out. It was so difficult and I was always treading on egg shells, trying to keep Dan from hurting my family and preventing my dad finding out that I was still seeing him.

I was on such a rollercoaster which I couldn't get off and my soul felt truly tormented. I had to lie to my mum and dad where I was going and spent most of my days at Dan's mum's house. So much lying, deceit and sneaking around and all just to avoid him get angry again.

I liked his mum, she was a gentle and kind person and my impressions of her was that she had lived a hard life. Even she, his own mother was scared of Dan, she would flinch when he lost his temper and gave the impression that she knew of his violent side and quench to control others.

She actually told me to get away from him. I even told her of what he was doing and asked her to help me. She put her head down in shame; she knew that I was trapped by her son's evil.

I got the impression that his dad treated his mum the same way. Reaching out certainly proved to be futile, I did this only once and it confirmed that there was no help out there for me.

Dan would take the last penny out of his mum's purse, leaving her to struggle financially. She didn't work so she was probably on benefits and sometimes Dan would take all of her money so he could go to the pub. She would still be expected to buy food and keep Dan supplied with cigarettes though. If she could not supply his cigarettes, he would really kick off with her and often she left the house in tears. He did not care about anyone but himself.

Within days, Dan asked me to move into his mum's house with him, he was convinced that this would be a good thing and that this would 'stop my family interfering'. I told him that my dad would not allow doing this, he called me so many horrible names and accused me again of seeing other men and used this as an excuse to exercise his evil nature.

On this occasion it resulted in him using my head as a hammer on the wall, he just kept banging my head on the wall using my hair as a grip, eventually I fell to the floor. I became numb to the physical pain he put me through even this attack didn't seem to hurt me, although my battered and bruised face would say different.

His words "You will do what I say, when I say. Do you want me to murder your family?"

I now had to agree to move in, at this point I wasn't bothered of what he did to me as he couldn't physically hurt me anymore, I was so used to his beatings and sex demands.

It was the threats of what he would do to my family that I cared about. I found every word he said was true and believed he would carry out his threats.

Later that day I went back home and packed a small bag, sneaking in and out of the house so that nobody saw me before going back to his mum's.

Around 10 pm that night someone was pounding on the front door, it was my dad. Dan ordered his mum to answer as he hid cowering behind the kitchen door.

My dad was fuming and demanded I got in the car or he would drag me in. He told Dan's mum that she should be ashamed of herself and that I was just a kid. He called Dan all the names under the son and told his mum she was just as bad "you dirty evil bastards".

I went to get my coat and Dan grabbed my arm and whispered to me so that my dad could not hear, "Go with him and sneak back later, you know what I will do if you don't, so don't dare let me down."

My dad was really ranting at me in the car, I just heard his voice and not his words, and all that was going through my head is that Dan will definitely kill my family now. Out of desperation I tried getting out of the car whilst my dad was driving, my dad quickly pulled me back in by my hair and coat. I so wanted to tell him what was happening but couldn't find the words and was too frightened of what the consequences would be.

When I got back home, my dad carried on ranting at me and eventually went to bed. I had to sneak out of the house by dropping about fifteen foot out of my bedroom window and arrived back at Dan's mums about two thirty in the morning to find him having sex with someone else.

I just stood there with my mouth open looking at them both and couldn't believe what I was seeing.

I certainly was not jealous, in fact I felt a sense of relief that he had found someone else and expected him to finish with me. He seemed shocked that I was there and quickly got rid of the girl but not before he made her feel like dirt, she left the house crying. Of course this was my fault for not being there when he needed sex, which he made clear to me.

The anger on his face was fearful. "You and your family have driven me to this," he blurted out after hitting me a few times. He grabbed an object and hit me over the head which knocked me out cold.

I must have been out cold for a few hours because it was daylight when I came round. No ambulance was called; I could have been dead for all he knew. When I came round he was sat on the floor next to me crying for what he had done and expressed how sorry he was, he blamed my dad for this, apparently 'he had no right coming to his house and having a go at his mum'.

He cuddled me and asked for my forgiveness, I told him that I was okay and 'forgave' him as I couldn't bear the thought of another beating.

My head felt cold and wet, I had blood coming from the side of my head and I felt the sick rise from the pit of my stomach. I went to the bathroom and washed away the blood so nobody could see what he had done. My hands were trembling as I watched the bloody water go down the drain, my head felt like it had been split into two and I held my hand over a part of my head because I thought my skull was falling out.

The remorse soon stopped and Dan told me that I had to convince my dad into letting him back in their home, his reason "You could be seeing other men for all I know!" He asked me what I was hiding, "Do you enjoy making me jealous?"

I knew what I had to do and eventually wore my dad down and he let Dan back in the house after me pleading with him. My dad questioned me about some of the bruises I had; I just made some excuse up like it was nothing.

About 12 months into the relationship from hell he asked me to marry him. We were at my parent's home when he 'proposed'.

I already had an engagement ring on my finger which had been slapped on weeks before by him. It was never a proposal, just another threat and another way to control me. When he slapped it on my finger he told me that I would never get away now.

I replied to his marriage request in the best possible way that came to mind at the time, "Why don't we leave it for a while as I am not ready for marriage and my dad wouldn't let me yet?" Straight away I regretted the minute these words came out of my mouth. He put his hands around my throat and squeezed that hard I passed out and wet myself.

When I came round, he kept saying "You belong to me. You can't say no. I told you, you're mine!" So I agreed to marry him and made excuses up for me previous rejection to his so called proposal.

I had to wear a scarf around my neck for weeks to hide the bruises around my throat and pacified this as fashion with my family.

He made sure I was dressed up to the hilts when he took me out to pubs and clubs like I was some sort of trophy. He would not think twice about fondling me in public which was a regular thing, regardless if anyone could see. He even had some of his friends sit with us whilst he did this. Sometimes he would find a quiet corner and make me do things to him, I will not go into detail about this and this wouldn't take much imagination to guess. Times like this were so humiliating and degrading for me, I was like a puppet with him pulling my strings and this was another depth of hell he took me to.

People would look at us and he didn't give a dam. The thoughts that were going around my head were, 'I want to die, I can't take this anymore, please god, help me!'

On one occasion when I was out with him at a club, the usual things happened but he got up and started dancing with a woman. His hands were all over her and I just sat there watching.

Something just snapped in my head and I got up and dragged her to the ladies by the hair with one hand and held an empty bottle in the other. I started screaming nonsense at her, calling her a slag amongst other names. I was dragging her head from side-side using her hair and then smashed the empty bottle on a sink and held the sharp end to her neck. My hand had blood pouring down from holding the rugged end of the glass.

Then I realised what I was doing and dropped the glass and apologised profusely to her. I didn't know what had come over me and why I did such an unforgivable thing, this is not in my nature.

I just ran out of the club crying and absolutely devastated for what I had done. Unsurprisingly, he came after me and thanked me for showing jealousy; he really got a buzz from this.

It wasn't jealousy that was my driver; it was me hitting the peak of insanity and truly losing control and insight because of his cruelty.

I think in my head, it was him that I was doing that to; I wanted him to be at the other end of the jagged glass. I wanted to cut his throat and if I could go back to that point I would have killed him given the chance.

I would often walk with my head down in shame, not daring to make eye contact with anyone. If another man looked at me, Dan would call me a slag and punish me later on.

He would always make sure that he hit me where the bruising and cuts could be hidden by clothing apart, except on one occasion where he used my face as a cheese grater on a brick wall, this took weeks to heel and I used the excuse that I had fallen on concrete steps, I always had an excuse for any bruising.

On another occasion when I made him angry, he told me that he was dropping me off at home but he had to put petrol in his car first. At the petrol station, he put fuel in his car and filled a petrol can.

I could tell how angry he was, I hadn't done anything, but if anything went wrong I would reap the consequences. He pulled up at my home but parked where nobody could see his car.

He looked at me in the eyes and asked me if I was sorry for upsetting him, although I still had no idea why he was angry. I apologised for making him angry to try and keep the peace and promised that I would not do this again.

When I got out of the car, he put his arms around me and told me he forgave me and then stated, "You will never learn, will you? You never listen." He got the petrol can out of the boot of his car and dowsed me with petrol; screaming at me, “How many times do I have to tell you so that you understand? If I can’t have you then nobody can you, thick bitch?” He took his cigarette lighter out of his pocket and started to toy with me, clicking the lighter so I could see the small flames. “Who will look at you when I burn you to a crisp?” he yelled. He continued to threaten me for around five minutes.

I begged and begged him not to do it, his reply to this “If I can’t have you, nobody can and don’t forget what I am capable of. This is your last warning!” He got in his car and drove off. I turned and ran into the safety of my parent’s house as quickly as possible.

My mum and dad were out but I could hear the TV on, there always seemed to be someone at home, very rarely would everyone be out. I went straight upstairs and jumped into the shower fully clothed to get the stench of petrol of me.

There were plenty of other occasions when he did similar things just to remind me that he was serious and I belonged to him.

He was banned again from my parent’s home and this was probably down to my changing behaviour with them. They would say that he was a bad influence on me but they remained clueless as to what he was doing to me.

Dan didn't seem that bothered at the time about this though, although he called my dad fit to burn. He wasn't upset because my parents didn't like him, he was angry because he lost some control.

Dan would often tell me to be ready at a certain time because he was taking me out and very often he didn't turn up. I would be dressed to the hilts on his demands and wait for hours looking out of the window for him to turn up. My family used to question this and I would tell them that I couldn't be bothered going out. I would have knots in my stomach and wonder what he was doing as I knew one way or another I would be punished for him not showing up.

On such occasions he would throw stones at my bedroom window for me to sneak him in, this would always be the early hours of the morning when he was drunk and had obviously been with someone else. Sometimes he would just lay into me and tell me that he had to have sex with someone else because he couldn't trust me. Other times he would make me have sex and do stuff to him; this was always violent and threatening.

The next day I would sneak him out of the house before anyone was up. Sometimes he would refuse to go so I had to sneak him some breakfast. He would say "I will fucking kill your dad if he comes in here."

On these occasions he would make me have sex again whilst my family were getting ready for work or moving around, all part of his plan for control. I would be at my wits end in case anyone came into the room. Then I would have to sneak him out later, he wouldn't be silent and seemed to thrive on the thought of getting caught.

After 18 months of being treated so cruelly, something snapped within me and from somewhere I got the strength to tell him that we are finished.

It was on a day that he came to my parents' home; he must have been watching and waiting for everyone to leave until he knew I was on my own. I opened the door to him, leaving him on the doorstep. I left the front door ajar and told him it was over and that he needed to get help. I was at a point in my life where I was past caring and had to do this, regardless of what the outcome would be.

I could tell by the look on his face where this was going, he glared at me and scrunched up his face getting ready to react.

I had planned what I would do before I opened the door and had prepared myself in a manner. I knew my actions could result in him killing me, but I had honestly convinced myself that if I ended up dead I would be in a better place.

I knew that if I didn't stick to it this time he would definitely kill me and my family and I was willing to let this happen, I just couldn't take any more of his cruelty.

My whole body was trembling and waiting for the consequences. Suddenly and unexpectedly, from somewhere I got the courage and strength to clench my fist and hit him in the face. I hit him so hard, he fell to the floor.

I couldn't believe that I had done it, I did not plan to do this and come to think of it I didn't really have a 'plan' when I first opened the door, any 'planning' I had done wasn't thought through and was in haste. Something must have really snapped in my head, it just happened.

I looked at him on the floor and saw a very different expression on his face. I remember thinking what have I done?

But the look on his face proved to me what a weak pathetic person he was. I ran into the house and locked the door behind me; my heart was pounding and my whole body was shaking. I sat on the floor cowering with my weight leaning on the door hoping I would be strong enough to stop any attempt from him to break in.

I kept thinking that one of my brothers or my mum would come home, and Dan would kill them. He opened the letter box and tried to peep in at me, he told me that I wouldn't get away with it and that he was going to kill me. He said he would 'turn up when I went to sleep, when I went out, and he'd be there ready with a knife to slit my throat and then one by one he would do the same to my family'.

People were passing by and being the coward that he was he walked away and got in his car, he was probably frightened of someone confronting him.

Physically and mentally I had had enough and couldn't go back regardless of the consequences.

I swore to myself that day that I would never go back to him despite his threats and promises of what he would do. I wanted my life back and I finally put an end to this.

For a few weeks after I finished with him, he would throw small stones at my bedroom window to get my attention; this was always in the early hours of the morning. I would peep through my bedroom curtains trembling and waiting for something bad to happen, but eventually he would give up and leave when he knew he could not get me to rise to his attempt to gain control over me again.

I still lived in fear of him for months and slept with one eye open listening for any noises, half expecting him to be standing in my bedroom with petrol or a knife. I was always alert and ready for him to attack me, even in my own home, day or night I kept expecting him. I would take a deep breath before I opened a closed door anticipating him to be there hiding.

At night I would check my wardrobe and under my bed and then wedge something against my bedroom door so he couldn't get in.

He must have realised that he could not get me back so he attempted to kill my dad by cutting the break pipes on my dad's car. Luckily my dad knew that his car had been tampered with and nothing came from this.

This action was out of desperation, his way of trying to regain control of me, and his way of telling me that he was serious and his threats were not just words.

I honestly believe that this situation would have escalated if I had have carried on in that warped relationship and his threats to my family would have for sure become real regardless if I was still seeing him or not.

For eighteen months I was raped, emotionally abused, mentally abused and physically abused. Not once did I give consent to sex and not from the first day I met him did I want to be with him.

It was endless, so much abuse. There are things that I haven't included because I just can't put them into words and they are far worse than the things that I have already revealed. Some things are better left unsaid.

My opinion of myself couldn't get any worse, all I can say is that I was unwilling and threatened into it.

My family had a good inclination that Dan terrorised me, especially towards the end. My dad knew that he was the one that cut his break pipes and I am sure that my dad would have confronted Dan about this without me knowing. My family are not the ones for calling the police; they would deal with any situations in their own way.

My brother Mark must have realised how scared I was of Dan after we finished. Mark saw me looking out of the upstairs window, peeping from behind the curtain. Dan was looking up at the house standing a few yards away, Mark caught on to this and casually went out and over to Dan and battered him.

I didn't go out of the house for a few months after finishing this relationship. I had it in my head he was waiting to get me. I told my family about him hitting me but was too ashamed to reveal anything more.

I did find out that not long after I left him, Dan dated another girl I distantly knew. She lived very local to me at the time. A few weeks into their relationship, he dragged her over half a mile by her hair and nearly scalped her. She later met with me and told me about her experience. Apparently, as he was dragging her, he was swearing at her and told her that she would 'never be as good as me'. This just shown that evil was in nature and that it wasn't my fault.

Eventually my friend talked me round to going on a night out with her and said that her brother would take us, stay where we was and bring us back home. She knew that I had been through an ordeal but still I couldn't confide in her or any other person, I felt so cheap and dirty.

This night out lead to a much happier chapter of my life, the night out changed my life and gave me a totally different direction. This was the night when I met my husband Bobby.

## *Chapter 5*

## *Love of my life*

I spent time getting ready for a well-deserved night out with my friend; I put on plenty of makeup and kept wiping it, I felt really unbalanced about doing myself up. I tried outfit after outfit on and each time I put something on I would change it. I didn't want to stand out and just wanted to look plain so nobody would look at me.

I was so nervous when I left my home and was certain that Dan would appear. I was so convinced that he would pounce out from nowhere or turn up where I was going. I tried to back out of the night out we had planned but before I knew it I was in the car with my friend and her brother. In the back of the car was another guy, he was a friend of my friend's brother

Bobby seemed very pleasant and chatted to all of us as we made our way to the club. When we arrived he sat with me and my friend and bought us a drink. My eyes were scanning the room looking out for Dan, I had an awful sense of dread like I was waiting for something horrific to happen, thinking he would murder anyone that is near me.

Although Bobby was nice, I had to ask him to move away from me and told him if my ex-boyfriend seen him sat with me, he will kill him, not that Bobby was making a move on me as he seemed really nice. I felt so defeated by Dan again, he was still controlling my thoughts and life and I was ready to go home as I couldn't bear the feelings I had.

Bobby asked who my ex was and when I told him he laughed and said he is not going anywhere. Bobby shouted one of his friends over and joked, "We need to be scared as Dan may turn up." They clearly both knew who Dan was and laughed. Bobby tried to reassure me that Dan is not a problem, and would stop him if he tried to come near me. Even though I kept telling Bobby that he would have no chance against Dan, he really would kill him, he didn't leave my side.

I latched onto Bobby as I felt at ease and that he would try to protect me, but still worried that Dan could destroy him as I knew more than anyone what he was capable of.

Dan did appear as I had thought he would and looked over at me and stared, it felt like he had turned me to stone.

I remember thinking that he was going to walk over to me and drag me away; I couldn't swallow or move as I was overcome by fear, I started to shake uncontrollably and couldn't find the courage to run. All the courage and effort I had put in to get rid of him seemed pointless. He still had this hold over me and felt that I was sinking back into the thoughts that he was still controlling me, making sure that his evil ways still impacted on me *a*nd that I could not have a life without him.

Bobby must have sensed this and went over to Dan, I'm not sure what was said but I could see the expressions on their faces. Dan looked defeated and starred at me as he left the building, the look on his face was so cold and his stern frown seemed like he was reminding me that there was no escape from him.

Bobby re-joined my friend and me, he told me I need not worry and Dan was out of my life for good. Although I felt partially reassured, I still had visions of Dan planning and scheming something outside club and was waiting for me. I could not enjoy the night out or relax, as far as I was concerned I had to be on guard anticipating how I could survive once I went outside.

Bobby tried his best to make me feel safe and I got on really well with him, it seemed like I had known him for years. The night started fairly dull and my anxiety impacted on this tremendously, but before long we ended up having such a laugh. It had been such a long time since I let go and truly laughed.

Bobby was a good influence on me and we had plenty of things in common. I didn't feel controlled or threatened by him, he had such a warm personality and seemed a very genuine person

In fact this night out was a start of something that developed into a beautiful relationship which led to us getting married two years later? Our relationship felt so right and normal.

We had so many things in common; we discussed normal things and communicated well with each other. We both made decisions on important things and our relationship became solid, I felt so happy and content. Finally something good has happened in my life.

Not long before we married I often questioned myself, is this really what I want, do I need to give myself more time. I didn't feel like a whole person, there was something missing in my life. I couldn't really fathom out what this was, but one thing for sure, I knew that I loved Bobby and we did get married.

I was fairly honest with Bobby about some of my experiences with Dan, when I spoke about my two years of hell. It was like talking about someone else and not me. The whole experience was a haze and felt so distant, I couldn't relate to me being that person.

This may sound silly but I considered myself to be a virgin when I met Bobby and could not show any emotion about my past. I was a nice girl and couldn't possibly be the girl that had that kind of history; I don't really know what made me think this. I obviously knew it happened but it was to a girl I once knew and not to me. This is probably called denial.

I couldn't remember the horrors of my childhood it was like I erased them from my head and did not give it a second thought.

Getting married to Bobby was the best thing I ever did, we had a big white wedding and the day went perfect. We have four beautiful children and an army of grandchildren and to date we have been married for 36 years. We have stayed loyal and our lives have been so good together.

There have been ups and downs from where I built a barrier where intimacy was concerned. We have a fairly normal husband and wife relationship, but often I found it hard to relax and enjoy a healthy sex life.

Subconsciously it has been my past that has had this effect on me. I have never spoken to Bobby about the impact of my past and how this affects me and sometimes this has caused some tension between us. We always got past this and this is because our relationship is so solid and strong.

I didn't really have or never really had any motivation or aspiration to do anything with my life and have never set any kind of career goals. I really enjoyed every moment of bringing my children up, there was never a day that I didn't give them every ounce of love I had.

My husband was the bread winner and I got a job working part time as a care worker. I didn't really have any qualifications from school; again I wasn't motivated and had never been encouraged to do well. I suppose coming from a family of seven children must have been hard on my parents and they were both raised as their parents seemed fit, education was not the top of the parenting list.

Jobs were much easier to come across back then and being a care worker allowed me to work around Bobby's hours and the children's school as they were my priority. I enjoyed my work and got great pleasure helping vulnerable people; I went above and beyond for them and sometimes would go back to them in my own time and do some shopping, decorating and even gardening. I was always offered extra money from them but would not take a penny. My reward was making life a little easier for them; I think I worked more voluntary hours than paid hours, Bobby used to laugh at this and at the same time admired me for doing this, but I got great satisfaction from this and never once moaned.

You couldn't go that extra mile in care work now as current legislation deems this as a safeguarding issue, back then there were no such laws that care organisations had to be compliant, there was very little guidance, rules and hardly no policies.

I worked for a few care agencies over the years and always got promoted fairly quickly and eventually managed companies and gained the relevant qualifications I needed.

I became a determined person with a desire to improve myself so that my children would be proud of me. I would concentrate on doing course work during the night and early hours of the morning, some nights I would not sleep. Managing a care service and having four young children was very demanding. I made sure that my children stayed as my priority as they were my world. I made time and even enrolled at college to gain further qualifications.

Every time my husband and I were off work at the weekends we would always be active and take the children out, this could be to the fairground, Delemere Forest, the beach or other places. We would go on holiday each year, sometimes in this country and other times abroad. We had lots of fun as a family wherever we ended up.

My children have always told my husband and I that they had a fantastic childhood with many good memories. Without a doubt these were the best years of my life.

When Bobby was thirty seven years old, he developed heart/lung disease; he worked for the NHS and ended up being admitted to the hospital where he became critically ill. He was on the coronary care unit and it was touch and go for a while. His health eventually improved and he was discharged from hospital.

A couple of weeks later he went back to work and ended up being admitted to coronary care again. This went on for months; he would recover, go back to work and end up being admitted again, it became a cycle for both of us.

Over these months, I worked full time in a high demanding job, managed to be there for my children who were all at primary school and visited my husband in hospital. Some nights/early hours of the morning I would prepare tea for the next day so that my children had healthy meals and would often work through the night trying to catch up with work.

I had to give up college eventually and looking back I don't know how I managed such a hectic life. I was always on the go and never give this a second thought. Bobby had to take early retirement from work and has never been able to work since.

This changed all our lives in a huge way, we became less active as a family as Bobby's health condition had to be taken into account. I became the bread winner of the family and had to make sure that that my earnings matched any outgoings we had.

We still made our children's lives happy and continued to go on holiday and days out each year but not as often as we were used too, still happy times with such good memories.

My husband's health deteriorated very often and there were countless times when I had to ring 999, worried that he would not make it, but he always bounced back.

Now, he is able to manage his health and knows his limitations, it is not as drastic as when he first got diagnosed although there are times when he has been admitted to hospital.

I worked very hard and became successful in developing a career that I am happy in, and on really good money. I have a very challenging job and has it stressful moments like most jobs.

My children have got their own little families now and visit on a regular basis with my grandchildren, in fact nearly every day of the week my home is filled with the sound of laughter and there is always one of them having tea with their little family. No matter how tired I am, I so much enjoy the noise and chaos that they bring.

But there was something deep within that prevented me from being truly happy and I could never quite put my finger on it. My life seemed to be hazy sometimes and there was something missing or not quite right.

My married life has been and still is happy but my past has had an impact and has prevented me from living the dream or living happily ever after. Some days I have felt depressed for no obvious reasons and have reacted to the normal ups and downs of daily life badly and may have gone over the top in the ways that I have handled some situations.

Other times I have felt like a lost soul desperately looking for the light, but during these years I suppose I just got on with it having no idea why I was feeling this way.

The experience with Dan seems like a fog and that it happened to somebody else, even though I have spoken about it having to face some of my experiences. It has always seemed that I was talking about someone else, showing no emotions. I just couldn't associate myself with being that person.

## *Chapter 6*

## *Let down*

When I started work as a care worker, I needed to have my own transport to get around the community. When my car broke and was beyond repair I was devastated as I couldn't afford a replacement. I was very close to my mum and dad and visited them almost daily. My dad had plenty of money and offered to take me to the car auctions and buy me a new car.

I was so grateful and offered to pay him back when I got some money but he insisted it was his treat. I can't remember where the auctions were and we looked at lots of different cars from bangers to sport cars.

We had breakfast when we first got there and spent a few hours looking at the cars, my dad got his handkerchief and said I had something on my chin and wiped it off. This seemed pretty strange as this was the sort of thing mum and dad did when I was a child.

My dad suggested that we leave the auction for an hour and go somewhere for lunch; I was pretty hungry and looked forward to a nice meal.

It seemed like my dad was driving for hours before pulling into a lay by. The area reminded me of the Yorkshire Moors. I asked him why he had pulled over and didn't think for a minute that there was any dramatic reason for this.

He switched off his engine and put his arm around the back of my seat and asked me how grateful I was. The way he asked me felt strange but I answered his question, "Dad I am really grateful and will pay you back." He came closer to me and out of the blue he asked me to show him how grateful I was. My facial expression of horror answered his question. I felt sick and started to tremble.

He went on the defensive and said he didn't mean it like that, I had got him wrong. He started his engine and drove to a restaurant and bought lunch. I starred at the food on my plate and felt sick to my stomach. I repeatedly asked myself, "Did that just really happen?"

I kept thinking to myself I got it wrong, my dad wouldn't do that, he's my dad. I asked him to take me home and said I didn't feel too well, he took me back to the auctions and brought me a car, it was a Charlton. I wasn't interested in the car; any excitement I had was destroyed and still doubted my judgement about what had just happened?

The day started with excitement and ended in a nightmare. I didn't get my dad wrong and knew exactly what he wanted from me.I couldn't believe what had happened. I have always looked up to my dad and had nothing but respect for him. This just crumbled my respect; how could he suggest something sexual? He is my dad!

I was married with four children, how could he put me in such a position, he is the grandfather of my children. I drove back to my home in my new car sobbing.

I told my husband about what had happened, he was blazing but I kept saying I must have got it wrong, my dad isn't like that and continued to make excuses up for my dad's behaviour.

I went round my parents' house the next day, my mum was over the moon that I had a car and yet my dad looked at me like he would normally look at me.

He spoke like nothing had happened. I kept going over it in my head and doubted myself. My dad isn't like that; I must have got the wrong end of the stick. The questions just carried on in my head and I desperately tried to think I did get it wrong.

But deep down I knew what he tried was real and I couldn't bear to bring this up, it would have destroyed my mum and the rest of my family so I just put it into the back of my head and carried on as normal.

I had always looked up to my dad, he had been a solid figure in my life and I had always respected him. His actions left me feeling so betrayed, like he had robbed me of my dignity. Nothing drastic happened but I know this was only because I stopped this in its tracks before this escalated.

The thought of what he tried to do destroyed me, someone who has always been stable in my life, a loving dad and a figure that I have always respected, how could he do that to me?

His negative and vulgar gesture ruined all of this, but I couldn't show this as the rest of my family would have picked up on it, especially my mum. So I kept quiet, I would not forgive myself if I destroyed my family, even though my own dad has put me in such a position.

I still sometimes doubt that my dad really did this, I keep going over this in my head but deep down I know what happened I just struggle to accept it happened.

## *Chapter 7*

## *Brother's funeral*

My beautiful mother passed away over twenty years ago. Her death really affected me, she was my best friend and it took me a long while for me to come to terms with this. Eventually the pain faded and the lost feeling was replaced with happier memories. I miss her so much; she would have loved having great grandchildren around her. She will never be forgotten and I have often spoken about her to my grandchildren, she was an amazing mum.

Life went on. I remained happily married and loved my family set up. My career is at its peak. I have worked hard to secure a good, responsible and happy career which has made me financially secure and enabled me and my family to live comfortable. I have stayed close to my brothers, sister and dad and we all get together at family events and always meet at my dad's on Christmas day.

In 2016 my brother Malcolm was rushed into hospital and put onto intensive care, we were told to prepare for the worst. I was devastated and could not believe my brother was so ill. I visited Malcolm almost every day and was genuinely upset to see my brother with so many tubes and wires hooked up to him as he lay there lifeless. As I looked at all the equipment in place that was keeping him alive and my brother, the frail man lying in the bed, I felt a knot in my stomach and I had a lump in my throat. I held his hand and the words just came out of my mouth, "I will never forgive you." I didn't want my older brother to die but since his admittance to hospital I had started to have flashbacks to what he had made me and my sister do. This was such an awful time and I was left with so many mixed emotions of what he did to his little sisters and the fact that he might die.

Eventually over a few weeks he started to improve and was taken off life support; he had to have a tracheotomy as he struggled to maintain his airway. He was transferred onto a normal ward, he was so weak, frail and still very poorly. I went through a period of panic and lived in dread in case he remembered what I said to him when he was on a life support machine, I was so worried.

Within a couple of weeks after being transferred he had the tracheotomy taken out and was able to talk. I could not hold back anymore and asked him if he remembered anything about his experience on life support and could he hear people talking. He said all he could remember was being in different rooms that were on fire and he couldn't get out. I felt relieved with this news as he did not hear or remember what I had said to him and I certainly did not want any eruptions or cause any fall outs.

I properly over reacted to what he told me about his experience whilst on a life support machine, as I jessed and told him that what he experienced was probably "hell". I was quite angry with myself for saying something so awful. I wanted him to recover and not suffer; after all he was my brother.

Eventually he was discharged from hospital and was able to go home. After this he was in and out of hospital and within a couple of months he unexpectedly deteriorated and suddenly died.

The news of his death ripped my soul apart, "My brother was gone". It wasn't just me his death had affected; my whole family were devastated by the news

I went through a short grieving stage which turned to frustration, guilt, anger and confusion. At the time, I did not know why I had such darkened feelings "What was wrong with me, my brother was dead." I became so agitated with myself and could not fathom out why I felt like this. I could only presume it was from the shock of his death, but something was really niggling at me.

Malcolm had married twice and remained married to his second wife until his death. It was his wife who arranged his funeral. It was an awful time, she caused a lot of upset within the family, excluding his two sons from his first marriage from getting involved with any arrangements, although some of this I could put down to her grieving. She seemed to have a thirst to try taking control regardless of how she made my nephews feel. When he was on life support, she just wanted power over others and would often comment and say that she is next of kin.

Nothing she did was in my brothers' interest. It was almost like she wanted the power over others. She made clear to his two sons that she was the only one that could ask the medical team about his progress and undermined anyone else that was close to him.

I was put in the middle of her need to have control and found myself mediating and keeping the peace, trying to prevent a full on family feud during these awful times which made me angry, upset and confused.

I would often ask myself why all the bickering, they all should be pulling together for my brothers sake and this should not be put on my shoulders. I cared about my two nephews and supported them with their emotional feelings and anger which their step mum had fuelled. I supported them during Malcolm's illness, death and helped them pick up the pieces after his funeral.

When the day of the funeral came; there was a huge turnout of friends and family. One of Malcolm's friends came over to me; he had his wife and daughter with him. Firstly he gave his condolences and then he started asking me general questions about me, what do I do, was I married, do I have children etc? This was a normal conversation and seemed like idle chit-chat so I responded to his questions like anyone else would do.

As we were talking his eyes locked onto mine, I could have died with the horror, I knew those eyes. I had a flash vision of how those eyes had had some horrible effect on me.

The box of horrors from my past that I had put a lid on and stored so deeply in my memories started to crack open. I could never forget his eyes, the penny finally dropped as my memory became clearer. He was the one that raped me when I was 10 years old.

I didn't know how to react to this, in my time of panic I carried on as normal, talking to him and his wife like long lost friends, my stomach felt like it was in knots and my whole body felt numb and shaky.

After the service at the church, it was time to bury my brother. So many tears from people who loved and cared about him. My feelings were of panic, confusion, anger and guilt. I felt like I had condemned my brother to hell with my words I said to him.

I was filled with visions of his coffin being lowered into the flames of hell. I truly regretted the words I said to him when he was in hospital, I loved him as my brother like I love all my other brothers and the very thought of him going to hell and knowing that I had wished this on him was unbearable. I just wanted him to be at rest and to go to heaven with my mum.

It was after the funeral when I really started to remember the horrors of my past and not just through flashbacks.

The lid on the box I had stored away so deeply in my memories for so many years became too full and the lid on Pandora's Box started to open and its contents slowly seeped out, poisoning my every thought.

At the time I thought I had had some sort of breakdown, my memories were too ugly to be about me. At first I just thought that the loss of my brother had just made me warped and affected my way of thinking, after all grieving effects people in different ways. Reality hit me hard as I discovered my memories were real.

## *Chapter 8*

## *Therapy*

My brother's death and funeral opened Pandora's Box, the hidden horrors of my past started to surface. Slowly and over a short period of time every memory from my childhood torment started to change and take over my life in a way that my existence became unbearable. I couldn't cope as my memories haunted me and to think that I thought my life was fairly normal. I

Started to remember the horrible events from my past; my brothers' funeral had triggered images in my mind that I had hidden away and not been able to face my entire life. I thought I was having a breakdown and could not grasp or differentiate what was real in my life.

I started to feel ill and felt so lost, snap shots of my past started to piece together, my poison memories became clearer as I put the pieces together. Both day and night my existence became consumed with so much anger, frustration and self-denial. Surely this is not my past, how could this be? Did this really happen to me? What kind of person am I?

I got to a stage in my life where I found living unbearable and often contemplated with the thought of suicide; I was in such a dark place. Acceptance of what others have done to me in my past and having to keep this to myself for so many years became all too much for me. It was only the guilt of knowing what I would put my family through if I did take my life and it would be them that had to deal with this and pick up the pieces, suicide was so tempting but not an option. This is such a negative thought but also felt like a desperate way out.

I started self-harming and became very distant from my husband, children and grandchildren and did not want them around me. I would never say this to them, but they must have picked up on how distant I was with them.

I carried on working and only seemed to be there in body, my mind was caught up in the nightmares from my past, I seemed to be reliving every moment.

It came to a stage where my past, present and future had just become entwined and could not differentiate what was real in my life. My life was in the balance of living or taking my own life as I continued to struggle with my conscience praying I would do the right thing so that my family would not have to suffer the consequences if I allowed myself to be defeated. I found it so hard to believe that I am that person that had been abused at such a young age.

I have always been a strong person who takes the knocks of daily life on the chin and deal with them. My situation was out of control, I couldn't think straight or function normally. I couldn't eat or sleep, my feelings for others were engulfed in shame and self-pity for myself. I just felt the need to walk away from anything or anyone that meant anything to me.

I had some lucid moments when I knew that something was badly wrong with me. At this point I knew that I needed professional help and plucked up the courage and made an appointment with my GP. I found it so hard to confide in anyone and felt that others would look down at me. I went to see the

Doctor and just told a small part of why I felt so low, I was shaking, crying and felt so vulnerable. This was one the most negative moments that I have ever experienced.

The GP made me feel like I was worthless; there was no concern, care or compassion. I was on the verge of suicide; the doctor heard my words but did not listen to what I was saying or my cry for help. I was given anti-depressants, told that I defiantly need counselling but there is a six month waiting list. I was given a crises card so I could contact and talk to someone if it was urgent and it couldn't wait. Then the GP told me to present myself at A & E if I felt suicidal, was he for real? I was made to feel like I was a time waster. I rarely visited my GP and the whole experience was so cold and negative. I felt in no mental state or motivated to present myself to anybody else.

As I left the doctors, I broke down crying walking through the waiting room, people were looking at me and I felt so overwhelmed with the negativity and remember thinking I had no choice and needed to end it knowing that I could not continue living my life like this.

Then I remembered I was covered by a private healthcare service through my work, I went home and got the paperwork and went back to my car. I was sobbing that much that the paperwork became soggy with my tears of desperation and I found it so complicated to understand who I had to ring, what would I say? Would I be judged?

Out of desperation I finally made the phone call, the person that I spoke to was very understanding and reassured me that I will get support, just hearing this made me feel a little better and I didn't have to divulge the ins and outs of my past, just give a brief overview.

I was emailed a list of therapists and I just started to ring all the numbers that were given to me and had to leave messages. I avoided ringing any male practitioners; I was convinced I would only feel comfortable with a female.

The first therapist that got back to me was a male practitioner, he worked in partnership with his wife, he asked me to give a brief reason why I needed support and then asked if I would be comfortable with seeing him. I sort of froze and was taken back, how was I going to tell a man what had happened to me? I agreed to see him out of politeness, not really intending to really see him at all.

I remember thinking to myself, what he would think of me if I told him what I have done? I tried to talk myself out of going to my first appointment. I felt ill and so desperate but I didn't want to set myself up so that I would be judged and experience the negativity I had from my GP. In my defenceless state of mind the last thing I needed was someone looking down at me, blaming me for what I had done, even though I blamed myself for what happened.

However, I have to say, me seeing this through is the best thing I could have done. I met with the therapist and he has been amazing with me, I would not be where I am now without his unconditional support, empathy and compassion.

My first session with my therapist felt negative as I talked about some of the things that have happened, it was like I was talking about someone else and daren't say too much as I didn't want to him to think of me as the dirty person that I am. He really listened to me and heard the words I was saying. When my first session was coming to an end he established a form of treatment for me.

He was honest and told me it was going to be a painful process. I was just relieved that I had finally spoken to someone about how I was feeling and was not made to feel ashamed and worthless.

I was still at to the stage where I was hardly eating or sleeping and lost any motivation to do anything as nothing made any sense to me. My existence had become so bad I had to confide in my manager at work and took a month off on the sick. My manager was so understanding and supportive.

My mind wasn't on the job and I couldn't make sense of my role, nor any anything else in my life. I would have panic attacks which got the attention of others at work and I couldn't bear the thought of anyone approaching me. I really couldn't handle any pity, my colleagues would ask if I was okay and I honestly thought they knew about my past. I would hear people whispering or laughing and automatically presumed they were talking about me.

This was down to my paranoia; I hated myself for being me and what I had become. I had been lying to myself most of my life; I am not the nice person that I have painted myself out to be. I am a dirty whore whose life is pointless and meaningless.

My mood sank lower and lower the flash backs become more vivid. I got to a stage where I would only go out of the house if I had to. I became so paranoid and thought that everyone knew what I was. If I had to leave my home at any point I would be prepared to be attacked. I didn't feel safe in my own home and I tried to keep my family at arm's length and didn't want to know any of them. What would they think of me if they knew the truth?

I started to have panic attacks daily, some more severe than others and when I got them really bad I thought I was dying. I developed chest pain, pins and needles, my skin would be clammy, and my heart would feel like it was racing and often got the feeling that I was going to pass out. The panic attacks would just come on without warning and sometimes without any triggers.

When my emotions got too much I would self-harm to bring myself back to reality and get away from my deepest dark thoughts I was experiencing. I would put a hot iron to my arm and do other similar things to myself. I did this to keep my thoughts away from suicide; it distracted me when I was at my lowest.

Sometimes my memories would come flooding back all at once and I felt like each person from my past was out to get me again and continue punishing me. I would feel like my past was the present and it was happening now and was unable to clearly recognise who the people were that had come back into my life.

Such visions were so complicated; they felt so real and were hard to digest. Other times a small memory would come back and it would be so intense I would feel like I was reliving my past. The experience became so real and so detailed, I could smell and feel their presence. I actually thought my life was so unbalanced and meaningless and that the rest of my life would just be an existence of horror and torment.

I have been seeing my therapist for over seven months now and see him on a weekly basis. I have had both negative and positive impacts from these visits. These experiences vary, based on the contents of the session.

Each session, he always asks me how I have been from the last visit. I sometimes lie to him about this and do not give true reflections on my emotions and negative thoughts. I am good at painting a smile on my face and papering over the cracks of horror and torment. Sometimes when I hit a low my thoughts are quite frightening and unhealthy, I found it so difficult to get myself away from such feelings.

For the first couple of months I did not tell my therapist everything as I feel that I was somewhat to blame for what's happened in my past and that somehow I had encouraged this sort of behaviour from others. The shame ate away at me, poisoning anything that could become positive.

I have confided in him over the months and have shared most of my past experiences with him which I thought I would never share. He has never passed judgement, raised an eyebrow or made me feel dirty. He helps me to understand and accept that what happened to me in my past. He has repeated told me that it is not my fault, and the fault of others who inflicted their psychopathic fantasies on me. He always emphasises that I was just an innocent defenceless child.

He has tried different forms of treatment with me, the main one being eye movement desensitisation and reprocessing (EMDR), whereby he uses lights or headphones. When using the light therapy, with my eyes I follow the light which is like a flashing beam and flashes from one side to the other. With the headphones, I listen for clicks going from one ear phone to the other (it sounds like a ticking clock). The main focus when doing this is to think about a worse point of what has happened to me. He will talk to me while doing this and then afterwards helps me to gain something positive about one of my experiences.

The main points I get from this is that I was just a young innocent child who was used by psychopaths and none of this is my fault. I would take these positive thoughts away with me and within hours the negativity engulfed my thoughts.

EMDR treatment seems to take you back to an unwanted memory and then gives you strength to gain something positive from this.

He has tried different ways of doing this but I have found the earphones are more effective. At first it is hard to engage with this treatment and it is important to cooperate fully for this to be effective. This experience triggers other lost unwanted memories which I find so difficult to process on my own. Although the positive progress from previous sessions started chipping away at my negative self-image.

Each time I have seen him I have recognised positive improvements, some which have changed my views on what has happened to me for the better. At the same time I experienced negative feelings and this is usually another horrible memory that has come out of Pandora's Box that has been triggered in some way. I find this side to the treatment disappointing and the reason being, just as I convince myself that everything (or most memories) are out in the open, something else will come flooding back. What comes to my mind is that the horrors of my past will be endless and become a continuous rollercoaster of torment for the rest of my life.

Normally after most sessions I would express myself with a text message or email and would tell him some of the horrible things that I had done as I couldn't seem to do this face to face with him because I felt so ashamed.

Eventually I started to open up to him during my sessions about what happened in more detail about different ordeals and started to feel stronger. I could see a light and became more positive that I can get through this.

I have built a really good relationship with him and he has gained my trust. He has always remained professional and shown nothing but empathy, understanding and positive interest in working out solutions. He listens and does not pressurise me to talk about anything I felt uncomfortable with and he talks about solutions on how to handle such feelings.

Sometimes I feel that I have to bear this cross for life and will never truly get over it. My past, present and future seem to be engulfed by memories that are destroying my existence and anything that means anything to me.

Other times, self believe will override my negativity and I get back a part of the strength to continue taking positive steps

I have nightmares most nights and when I do go to sleep these nightmares seem like a reality and that I am back reliving my past experiences. I have such awful flashbacks and sometimes find it hard to come back and often get confused of what is real.

One night I woke up convinced that I was on fire and all I could smell was burning flesh. I realised that this was a nightmare from the day Dan dowsed me in petrol. The weirdest part about this is that I could actually smell petrol on myself for a couple of days, regardless of how many times I showered and sprayed perfume. I was half expecting Dan to appear with a lighter; it felt so real and like it is happening now.

On a visit with my therapist, I told him what my brother had done because I was having such awful nightmares. I truly believed that I was being haunted by Malcolm; I went through weeks where he would come to me in my sleep and repeatedly told me to 'keep my fucking mouth shut'. I would wake in such a state and start with a panic attack. When this happened, I had to get up and clean the house or do something to take my thoughts to a better place but at the same time I was half expecting to see dishes flying across the room, my heart would be thudding and would have to do something extreme to make me realise that it was just a dream.

My therapist and I talked this through and came to the conclusion why I was experiencing such things and this was mainly because the death of my brother death triggered Pandora's Box to open.

Although I realised that the horrors of my past, are in my past and not happening now, my thoughts are nearly always impaired with the negativity of my past. When leaving one appointment, after talking about my dreams of Malcolm, the heavens opened when I walked to my car. There was so much rain and I thought it was a sign from my brother because I let his dirty little secret out. Triggers like this, makes me think that my past is now and that I should not have discussed my brother.

On recent sessions we have talked about my experiences, he has made it clear that I am the innocent party and what my brother, his friend, and Dan did to me is evil. My therapist has such a calming and reassuring voice and I always absorb what he says to me. He has planted a positive seed and continually grows positivity in me.

Sometimes, I am screaming inside and feel so knotted up and wish I could express myself when I am feeling this low. Instead I will talk and even laugh about something that are not relevant or do something silly. I find it so hard to let my emotions go and use anything to distract me when I am at breaking point with this. I just don't know how to react when my tensions build up through frustration, anger, fear, guilt and the unrealism of my experiences.

I feel that I am slowly accepting the fact that the experiences of what happened to me during my childhood and teenage years are not my fault and that my brother set a pathway for me in life to accept what was coming and to remain quiet.

The way he influenced me as a child, controlling my thoughts with his threats and casting a cloud of fear over me for so many years contributed and led to a continued pathway of being controlled and abused throughout my teenage years.

If he had not raped and threatened me at such an early age, maybe the other abusers in my life would have not have happened or maybe I would have been able to tell someone at the time so that they were punished.

What I do find very difficult is the mental scars which will always be there and the way that my body has been violated so many times. I feel that this is now causing me so much heartache; I can't seem to cry nor shed any emotions about this. I can clearly talk or write about what I was made to do, but feel like I have a time bomb ticking inside me waiting to explode and I still don't quite know how to handle this.

I can remember virtually every detail of the rapes and other abuse, I can sometimes, even now, feel the physical and emotional pain of what I felt then. These thoughts often come to me when I go to bed at night and always impact my sleep.

Sometimes in the daytime, my thoughts will be triggered by some reminder of my past; this could be a place that I have visited, driving past a river, seeing someone that looks similar to the faces of my past. These triggers can often cause me to panic and puts me back as being the terrified little girl again.

Fairly often, I will silently tell myself that if I can't take it anymore, especially when I am in a dark place 'suicide is an option and may be a way out'. This may sound selfish as I have my family to think about and their feelings, I really try to get my thoughts away from this but sometimes I just cannot get passed it. I suppose I have a hidden strength that has prevented this from happening.

My therapist is so good to me and will always answer his phone, ring me back or reply to any messages if I needed his support; he has a way of bringing me to the here and now and making me see sense.

On some occasions I have contacted him and attempted to cancel further appointments as I have convinced myself that nothing would fix me or my situation. He has never given up on me and had a way of making me see that I am making progress and would indirectly convince me to continue.

As far as I am concerned he has gone above and beyond to help me and has saved my life in more ways than one. I will be indebted to him for the rest of my life for the support he has given and is still giving me.

I am so happy and relieved that I am being supported and honestly dread to think of where I would be now without this support. I am at a stage where I know I am getting better and can see that I have made progress. My life is feeling more positive in so many ways. I know that I still have a journey ahead of me to getting to a stage of acceptance and self-belief.

Fairly often I feel that I am on top of this and then I end up taking two steps back as something else will come to mind from my past that causes me to hit rock bottom again. In my heart I know I will beat this and will not let the scum that has invaded my life destroy my future “I am a survivor and will not be a victim”.

## *Chapter 9*

## *Success*

My therapist has made me realise that I am a strong, unique person and that I defy all text books surrounding circumstance like mine. Usually other people that have had traumatic events in their lives have often turned to drugs and alcohol as a coping mechanism and their lives turns to a mission of self-destruction because they simply cannot cope.

Maybe I have been spared this to enable me to show others that there is hope and they can take back control of their lives.

I realise that I have lived in a shadow of my life for so many years and this is down to what happened to me as from being a child and how I somehow blamed myself. There is only so much that you can hide away and sooner or later we have to face our fears to enable us to move on and live a happier life.

You see, there are many people out there who do not understand what an impact such abuse has on someone's lives.

Maybe I could have walked away from the situation with Dan much earlier. I know now that what my brother did to me and the way he made me keep quite at such a young age set a deep fear inside which set a pathway in my life to keep silent and take what was coming or reap the consequences.

I honestly thought from my childhood and through to my teenage years that the damp patch on my bedroom ceiling was the devil. This image was waiting for me to divulge the dirty dark secrets that I was told to keep silent about and it was waiting to get me if I told anyone, this image kept growing as a constant reminder.

I know this was my imagination, but it is how my brother silenced me that created this horrible, fearful vision that was always a focus point for me.

For each time something happened to me, the devil's face became more detailed and life like. Inventing a clear vision of the devil's face at such a young age has also added so many traumas to my life.

The hidden past that I stored in Pandora's Box and buried so deep is because I was too frightened to tell anyone, and I suppose the fear is why I subconsciously blocked these events out of my life for so many years.

My brother's death was overwhelming and meeting the man at my brother's funeral that abused me when I was ten years old was too much. I had hidden my past away for some many years because I could not face, nor find the strength to do anything; it is like I deleted them and had no recollection.

There is only so much a person can hide away in the deepest parts of their memory and when there is no more room, Pandora's Box will become to full and the lid will come off.

We have to face our fears at some point in our lives and some of these fears may be soul destroying. The only way forward is to take a step back first. You will learn to eliminate the negativity from your past and learn where to get the strength from to take control of your own future and destiny.

The part in which I mentioned about never feeling like a whole person and always thinking there was something missing from my life. I have come to the conclusion that the only thing that was missing was my courage to face and challenge my past.

Since all my memories have come flooding back, I often say to myself that I want the happy ever after ending and don't deserve a life of misery and pain. I realise now that I have got the happy ending and have had this from the day I married Bobby, the love of my life. My success in life has flourished, still married and have been for thirty six years, I have four wonderful children and an army of grandchildren.

Bobby has been so supportive over the last months and I have been able to confide in him and talk to him about most upsets and negative feelings I have. He has picked me up when I have been at my lowest and has helped me to get through this in many ways.

Of course my past has affected my relationship with my husband, we have had times of passion and times that I have felt overwhelmed.

I have fairly recently spoken to my sister about our past and asked her if Malcolm raped her. I have found out that he did attempt rape with her but she was at an age where she knew this was wrong and told my mum and dad.

I have also spoken to my brother Mark and he knew that he tried to rape my sister. He told me that my dad went berserk with Malcolm and that he had to see someone professional about this. Mark also said at this time that my dad asked Malcolm if he had done anything to me or my sister and Malcolm swore blind that he hadn't.

My brother Mark said that he would never leave me and my sister alone with Malcolm because he thought that something might be going on. Now I know this information, I find it really hard to understand how Malcolm did this to me and got away with it.

If you think about the situation back then, why did nobody approach me and ask if Malcolm did anything to me? Why did no one care enough about me?

If my brother Malcolm was alive today, I would confront him about what he did. He would probably deny what he had done, but unfortunately I will not get that opportunity and this cannot happen now.

He set the pathway in my life to take what comes and be silent. He set his five year old baby sister up to have a life of misery and torment. I will never forgive him.

Ben, another rapist, preyed on vulnerable little girls with his psychopathic tendencies. I am unsure if it is just me he raped or if there were others, most probably there were. Ben has a family of his own now and I just hope that he is tormented by what he did to me.

Dan had a horrible impact on my life; I was trapped in such a horrific existence. He has obviously got something wrong with him for his behaviour to be so evil. It is just unfortunate for me that I ended up with him in my life and wasn't strong enough to do anything about it. He is a psychopath and should be locked up for good.

My Dad whom I had always respected, his actions on the day of that auction sickened me to my stomach, even though his attempt to do something that day did not go any further.

Just the thought of what he wanted to gain and being such a respected figure in my life destroyed me more than I can say. He is elderly now and I continue to visit and do things for him, but certainly will never respect him.

As I have been writing this, I realise how lucky I have been to have private healthcare. My therapist has made my life much happier and I can see clearly the improvements that I have made, I still feel that I have a lot to still come to terms with. The main thing is that I am slowly taking back control of my life and this is all down to the support and encouragement of my therapist and my husband.

If it was left to the support of my doctors I know that I wouldn't be here now. For me, there is no support what so ever apart from prescribed pills which only treat the symptoms and not the cause.

This has really got me thinking about how many people are out there who may have experienced similar things or just one what I have experienced. What help have they got? Would they benefit if they had some support to help them deal with their demons?

I have been to hell and back and have never relied on drugs or drink as a way out. What I have in life is unique, happily married with my own little family. I have a job that I have progressed in and made a good enjoyable career for myself and I am on good money. I am working on putting my life back together which I will fully achieve.

# Chapter 10

## Conclusion

I am fortunate and had the professional support that is enabling me to get on the road of recovery. Although I am still not a hundred percent better yet, I am at a stage where I know that I am going to be able to put this behind me.

Being raped, physically and mentally abused for so many years with the attempted murders is traumatic. Punishing and blaming myself throughout the years and being led to belief it is my fault. I now know that none of this was my fault and I was just an innocent child who was unfortunate to fall into the hands of psychopaths.

I for one certainly know that there is very little support out there for people who have suffered traumatic events in their lives. I know there are rape crises centres, The Good Samaritans and properly other help groups. There seems to be nothing for others who have suffered in silence traumas that they cannot come to terms with. Some will rely on alcohol or drugs to get them through each day. Why can't they be helped?

Nowadays sexual abuse is really hitting the media and famous people are being discredited by people coming forward and saying "rape". Usually if they get found guilty, the so called victim will get compensation. I often ask myself if such acquisitions are right, why anyone who has suffered would want to be the highlight of the media. Are they doing this to gain accreditation, fame, money? What about the people who are real victims and have had to face situations on there on their own, don't these people matter!

I truly feel that the cases that have been in the public eye and that have targeted famous people has cast a shadow on the reality of the meaning of "abuse".

There seems a lot of support for child abuse nowadays which is excellent, back in my days there was nothing. I don't think families could face the shame, so such abuse was swept under the carpet and ignored.

I have gone to hell and back over the recent months and had to face all my demons, I have had to relive all my horrific experiences which is enabling me to analyse my past and take positive steps to take control and not let what they did to me destroy what I have become.

I now realise I am strong person and always have been and this is why I am a survivor. A victim has been defeated and has not found the strength to deal with their darkness; most have turned to drugs and alcohol for comfort.

I am a successful business woman who has a successful marriage and four fabulous children. Of course I have a past, but this is what exactly what this is “my past”. My present and future will always be affected by the monsters of my past but I realise that none of this was my fault.

Moving forward, they will certainly not be in a place in my life where they can do anymore damage to me. I am in control and my life is a success, they have all failed and they have got to live with their evil ways and die without forgiveness, they will eventually get what they deserve.

All my tormented experiences have now given me so much passion and motivation to help others in getting the support they need and deserve.

## *Chapter 11*

## *What I want now*

What do I want after sharing my experience?

I want to set up a charity as a walk in centre and referrals from GP's. I don't want anyone to experience the negative attitude I had went I went to see my GP when I was in such a desperate state.

The cure for such experiences is not just medication, this does not work on its own as it will only treat the symptoms, and professional support is needed to treat the cause.

What can you do to help???

Personally I would not know where to start in setting up such a charity. I will need professional support to set this up from someone who understands current legislation around mental health. I know I will need money for premises and other expenses. I know trained professionals are needed who are qualified to help people to kick the alcohol and drugs. Other trained professionals who are able to offer a package of support.

I want a clear pathway created so that from referral, a plan of treatment will be established. The plan will be based on the individuals needs and there treatment will be monitored and action plans put in place to prevent the individual giving up.

I don't want any individual being turned away, even if this means signposting to somewhere else.

I want success rates!

I certainly want to raise more awareness of approaches to mental health needs, especially GP's who are mainly the first contact.

What will be gained?

The support I have had and still getting has been a life changing event for me and this has given me the passion to help others who have been less fortunate. In my experience, doctors seem to avoid mental health problems and just treat the symptoms by giving anti-depressants, sleeping pills and beta blockers etc. These symptoms will escalate unless the cause is being treated, but this cost too much money and there are not enough resources.

By having such a charity, others can be assessed and their mental health needs can be addressed by someone who cares enough to help them come to terms with a traumatic events and receive the support to help challenge and change their lives.

Everyone deserves the opportunity to access support and be supported to set positive goals. The outcomes would become financially better for the NHS as they would not be in a position where they are paying out for unnecessary medication long term. As for the individuals, they could become happier and be able to set themselves goals in life rather than self-destruct and end up with nothing.

There is very little support to help adults who have been abused when they were children and most are unable to face their fears, just like me. I have often thought suicide as an option to end such distress. I have got support to deal with these feelings and I can honestly see the light. I should imagine the suicide statistics are higher for people who have had such traumas without support.

For anyone who is reading this and in a position where you can help me set up such a charity, this could be by simply donating money or have the professionalism to involve the right people to engage in this.

We all know someone that will benefit from this and with your support there will be so many life's that will be changed.

This is giving the opportunity for you to step up, save life's and promote more understanding about mental health which isn't promoted enough.

It is not just women that get abused; there are plenty of men who have experienced this. They need the support and resources to help them understand and come to terms, the support to get off the alcohol or the support to get off the drugs.

Having a charity that can offer different pathways of support to help them in these areas can make a difference.

Please don't sit back and read this and do nothing! Give others a chance in life!

Have the professional abilities?

Are you in a financial position?

Do you just want to help and be involved?

Then please do something, help me to help others that are tormented!

Who knows, your support may make you become famous, and what a way to get your name known.

This book of pain is about true events of a little girl who endured rape, violence, emotional torture and attempted murder.  The torture was not by the hand of one person, but several. Her pain remained that well-hidden; it was only the death of one of her abusers that blew the lid of Pandora's Box when she became middle aged.

So many hidden black secrets that she found unbearable to speak of led her to a life of pure misery and pain.

She now has taken back control of her life, putting the psychopaths back into the past where they belong. Beating the emotions and blackmail of keeping quite has made her now realise that none of this was her fault.

She is determined to not let her past break who she is now. This is an unforgettable account how a middle aged woman has battled from the depths of hell.

Printed in Great Britain
by Amazon

48307908R00083